Character Counts!

40 Youth Ministry Devotions From Extraordinary Christians

by
Karl Leuthauser

D1166289

Loveland, Colorado

Dedication

To Gina, Madilyn, and Moriah as our story unfolds.

Character Counts!

Credits

Editor: Amy Simpson
Creative Development Editor: Jim Kochenburger
Chief Creative Officer: Joani Schultz
Copy Editor: Bob Kretschman
Art Director: Kari K. Monson
Cover Art Director: Jeff A. Storm
Cover Designer: Becky Hawley
Computer Graphic Artist: Joyce Douglas
Illustrator: Dave Klug
Cover Photographer: Index Stock and Craig DeMartino
Production Manager: Peggy Naylor

ISBN 0-7644-2075-5

10 9 8 7 6 5 4 3 2 1   08 07 06 05 04 03 02 01 00 99

Printed in the United States of America.

Contents

Introduction

"Did they tell you stories 'bout the saints of old?
stories about their faith?
They say stories like that make a boy grow bold,
stories like that make a man walk straight."

—Rich Mullins

Our Sunday morning youth program was set up like a small cafe. After worship in the auditorium, about two hundred teenagers would find their way to our meeting room, grab something at the "snack shack," and sit around the fifty small tables in the room. Because I was a volunteer who led the junior high midweek program, I didn't have to worry about giving the sermon or preparing the announcements. I could just mingle and connect with the teenagers—and more important, I could watch and learn.

The youth pastor was a dynamic speaker who had unparalleled passion for youth and for Christ. But the distractions of the cafe format coupled with the length of the sermon made it difficult for all the teenagers to completely pay attention. Sometimes the pastor commanded the attention of the entire room. Other times, the distractions proved too much, and the pastor had to interrupt his sermon to regain control.

One Sunday, when a youth ministry intern was speaking, I came to understand one of the factors that made the difference between complete interest and complete apathy on the part of the teenagers. The intern certainly had the desire to help the teenagers, but she wasn't a seasoned speaker. As her talk went on, the teenagers became less and less interested. The intern had almost lost complete control until she said, "I want to read part of a story to you."

She began reading an allegorical portion of *The Voyage of the Dawn Treader* by C.S. Lewis. In the story, a boy named Eustace had been turned into a dragon. A lion named Aslan peeled the layers of dragon skin off the boy. As I watched, I was amazed to see the teenagers listening and looking with rapt attention.

As the months went on, I continued to watch. Of course, there were many factors that led to an attentive or inattentive crowd. But I noticed that whenever a *story* was told, the teenagers *listened*. Guest speakers came to share their personal stories, and not a word of the stories was missed. The youth pastor would offer small stories about his own life, and everyone listened carefully as he spoke. I discovered, as you may already know, that stories have power.

Stories command attention because they draw people in on an emotional level. People want to know what others have gone through, how others have survived, and how others have felt. Stories help people see that they aren't alone in their struggles and desires. It's no wonder that God inspired men to record the stories of Israel and our salvation. The jealousy of Cain. The grumbling of the Israelites as God provided for them in the desert. The hesitant faith of Gideon. The wonder and amazement of Mary. The frustration of our Lord with his disciples in the garden. The parables of Jesus. God's stories, like many stories, are timeless. They connect with the reader and make an impression that is not soon forgotten.

Character Counts! 40 Youth Ministry Devotions From Extraordinary Christians is a collection of forty true stories you can include as part of your teaching or as the central part of a devotion you lead. These true stories come from the experiences of forty different Christians who have suffered, labored, and succeeded in the name of Christ. None of the women and men in this book were perfect. But every person tried to serve Christ with what he or she had been given. And for reasons known only to God, the actions or circumstances of these people have made them prominent characters of Christian history.

Their stories will inspire your students to live with character and will challenge your teenagers that Christlike character is possible and necessary. Your students will hear of a man named Maximilian Kolbe, who had the selflessness to offer his life in place of another man at Auschwitz. They'll hear about a woman named Mary McLeod Bethune, who was resourceful enough to overcome the Ku Klux Klan. They'll listen and be changed as you tell about a man named Abraham Lincoln, who found peace in a relationship with Christ. Your teenagers will see that others who have gone before them have chosen to live with character and that they can follow the examples of these great—yet very human—Christians.

Today's teenagers are desperate for role models and heroes. The devotions in this book will help them see that there are people who have lived and still live with integrity, selflessness, service, and other characteristics that should set us apart as Christians. Each story connects with a character trait such as wisdom, hope, endurance, or patience. The stories will challenge your teenagers to raise the standard of their own personal character while encouraging them to persist in faith and relationships with Christ.

And your teenagers won't be left to figure out how the stories apply to their lives. Each story is followed by a learning experience that gives students an opportunity to discuss the story, investigate what the Bible says about the character trait, and determine how the character trait can play out in their lives. The learning experiences are designed to be age-appropriate, engaging, and interesting. Your teenagers will actively participate in the learning experiences and will have the opportunity to draw their own conclusions.

I've found that the stories, Scriptures, and learning experiences in this book have challenged my apathy and encouraged my faith. I pray that *Character Counts! 40 Youth Ministry Devotions From Extraordinary Christians* serves as an effective tool God will use to change the lives of your teenagers as well as your own life.

Availability
Anthony of Egypt (250–355)

Read the following true story aloud to your students, or ask a student to read it aloud.

Anthony was born in Egypt in 250. He was a man of great faith as well as great wealth. As he studied the Scriptures, Anthony was challenged by Jesus' teachings on money. He read the story of the rich ruler in Luke 18:18-30—Jesus told the man to sell everything, give it to the poor, and follow him. He read Jesus' commands in Luke 14:25-33—to give up everything it took—including family, if necessary—to follow Christ. After reading these passages, Anthony faced a crisis. He believed he had to decide between wealth and Christ.

So Anthony chose Christ. He gave away his money and became a solitary monk in the desert near his home. In the desert, Anthony prayed, fasted, worked, and struggled with temptation. While he was there, he gained a small following of people who looked to him for instruction on living a life of holy poverty and solitude.

In the desert, Anthony learned what it means to endure hardship, to have nothing, and to be devoted to Christ. As he was growing in his devotion to Christ, Anthony felt God direct him to leave the desert and go to Alexandria. He went to boldly tell others about Jesus and to volunteer his life for martyrdom. But no one was interested in killing Anthony. The Roman persecution had ended, and Anthony's requests to die for Christ were ignored.

Feeling frustrated and a little confused, Anthony returned to the desert and eventually moved to a mountain where he prayed, fasted, raised a garden, and spent most of his time alone. In his later years, Anthony wanted only solitude and hardship. He said Christians in any setting must decide what kind of virtue they will reflect in their lives.

Sidelight

Anthony of Egypt is the father of Christian asceticism. Christian asceticism is physical self-denial and mental and emotional discipline for the sake of spiritual goals.

(Adapted from Holy Company: Christian Heroes and Heroines *by Elliott Wright.)*

Discussion Starter

Ask:

- **What's your opinion of Anthony?**
- **Do you think God was pleased that Anthony made himself available for martyrdom? Explain.**
- **What does it mean to be available for God?**
- **Should we make ourselves available to God in the same way Anthony did? Explain.**
- **Share a time when you were available for God.**
- **Share a time when you were unavailable.**

Have a volunteer read Isaiah 6:8-10 aloud.

Ask:

- **What was the result of Isaiah's availability?**
- **How can you follow Isaiah's example?**
- **What is God calling you to?**
- **Are you available?**

Sidelight

During one of his two trips to Alexandria, Anthony preached against Arianism. Arians taught that God the Father and God the Son were separate rather than united in the Trinity.

Say: **God can and will use the ability and talent he has given you. But God is more concerned with your availability than your ability. Anthony may have been misguided in the implementation of his availability. He probably didn't need to volunteer to give his life to people who didn't want to take it. But Anthony had one thing right—he was available to do whatever he thought God was directing him to do. Will you follow Anthony's example?**

Give teenagers an opportunity to put their words into action by providing them with a sign-up sheet of works of service your church needs help with. For example, you could list things like "help teach children's Sunday school," "help organize the retreat," "help clean the church grounds," and "give rides to other group members." Make sure there are more than enough works of service for everyone to choose from. Then pass the sign-up sheet and a pen or pencil around the group.

Compassion

Squanto (birth date unknown; died 1622)

Read the following true story aloud to your students, or ask a student to read it aloud.

Squanto of the Patuxets tribe was a strong and proud man when he was captured in 1605. Many European captains came to America looking for gold and other riches. After trading with the American Indians, some of the captains would kidnap young men. They would take these young men back to Europe as prizes for kings and queens who financed their voyages or to sell them as slaves. Squanto was captured by one of these captains and taken to England. But Squanto was resourceful and intelligent. It took him nine years, but he eventually escaped and returned to his village by traveling with an English fishing expedition. He was reunited with his land and his people.

But the happy homecoming didn't last long. Shortly after returning, Squanto was tricked by a man named Captain Hunt. The captain talked Squanto and other Patuxets into going aboard his ship. Once they were on board, the captain and his men ambushed and captured the Patuxets. Hunt then took the men to Spain and sold them as slaves.

Fortunately, Squanto was sold to Spanish monks. The monks helped Squanto with European languages and taught him about Christianity. After a short time, the monks gave the determined Squanto the opportunity to go back to London, where he was able to find passage back to America once again! With tremendous expectation and relief, Squanto returned to his native country. But when he came to his home village, he found that all his people were gone or dead—the tribe had been destroyed by a plague.

In 1621, when Squanto encountered the Pilgrims who were trying to establish a colony in Plymouth, he had every reason to hate them and all white people—as did many of the American Indian tribes in what would someday be the northeastern United States. But even though he had lost loved ones and was twice

Sidelight

Before encountering the Pilgrims, Squanto was taken in by the Wampanoag tribe. Squanto, along with the Wampanoags, attended a feast the Pilgrims prepared to give thanks for a bountiful harvest.

taken to a land he wanted no part of, Squanto chose not to act in hate.

After being introduced to the Pilgrims who had come to Plymouth on a ship called "Mayflower," Squanto made an amazing choice. He saw that the Pilgrims were unfamiliar with the land and that they needed help if they were to survive. And Squanto had compassion toward them. He chose to stay with the men and women of Plymouth. He taught the Pilgrims how to plant corn, stalk deer, and plant pumpkins. He showed them which herbs they could eat and which herbs could be used for medicine. Because of Squanto's instructions, the Pilgrims survived the winters and established a successful colony.

(Adapted from The Light and the Glory for Children: Discovering God's Plan for America From Christopher Columbus to George Washington *by Peter Marshall and David Manuel.)*

Discussion Starter

Ask:

• **Would you have treated the Pilgrims the same way Squanto did? Explain.**

• **Why do you think Squanto had compassion toward the Pilgrims?**

Say: **I believe you're all compassionate people. I also believe I may know the one thing that sometimes prevents you from acting on your compassion. You believe the little lie that says, "Someone else will do it." God doesn't expect you to do everything, but God does expect you to do something. If you believe someone else will do it, you'll end up doing nothing.**

Distribute Bibles. Say: **I'd like you to read Isaiah 58:6-10. When you're finished reading, mentally walk through yesterday. Start with the time you got up and finish with the time you went to bed. As you're thinking about your day, try to remember every person you saw who needed help or compassion. Then honestly think about how you responded. When you're finished reviewing the day, spend some time in prayer, asking God to show you who needs your compassion.**

When teenagers are finished praying, give volunteers an opportunity to share. Support anyone who

Sidelight

During the winter of 1621, the Pilgrims of Plymouth entered a time of famine, when each person was allowed only five kernels of corn a day. A ship headed from Virginia to England unexpectedly stopped in the harbor near the colony. The captain of the ship agreed to trade his corn for beaver pelts. Fortunately, Squanto had already introduced the Pilgrims to the beaver trade, and the colonists avoided starvation.

needs help with prayer. Then say: **Squanto had every right to walk away from the Pilgrims. He was the last person who should have showed compassion to them. But Squanto didn't believe the little lie. He knew he was the only one who would help. Next time you see a person in need, don't believe the little lie, and don't walk away.**

Conviction

John Bunyan (1628–1688)

Read the following true story aloud to your students, or ask a student to read it aloud.

John Bunyan couldn't turn his back on the calling God had given him. He was a preacher, and he had to remain faithful to God and to those he instructed.

Unfortunately, the king of England had ordered all Nonconformists—people who weren't part of the Church of England—to refrain from preaching. And Bunyan was a Nonconformist.

King Charles I had been killed in an English civil war, and the Nonconformist preachers and Christians had much to do with his overthrow. His successor, Oliver Cromwell, was much more sympathetic to the cause of the Nonconformists. But when Cromwell died, Charles II took power. Charles II was afraid the Nonconformists would preach against him and his authority, sending the country into another civil war. So no one was allowed to preach unless officially endorsed by the Church of England. Anyone else who stood before a gathering of five or more would face prison or banishment.

Bunyan ignored the declaration. He continued to preach because he believed God had called him to do so. During one of his sermons, Bunyan noticed the authorities gathering at the back of the assembly, waiting to arrest him. He could have simply disbanded the meeting and escaped. But Bunyan was true to his call, saying, "If I should now run and make an escape...what will my weak and newly converted brethren think of it? But that I was not so strong in deed, as I was in word." So Bunyan was arrested and taken to prison.

Sidelight

John Bunyan's jailer allowed him to leave his prison cell from time to time to preach to secret assemblies. Then Bunyan would voluntarily return to his prison cell.

While in prison, Bunyan agonized over his family. His wife, Elizabeth, was left by herself to care for their four children. Bunyan was especially concerned for his oldest daughter, Mary, who was blind. Bunyan described the separation from his family as "pulling the flesh from my bones." Despite the anguish Bunyan faced, he could have been released at any time if he had simply promised to stop preaching in unlicensed assemblies. Despite the simple and tempting solution that was always before him, Bunyan refused to turn his back on the call God had given him. He couldn't make the promise, and he stayed in prison for *fourteen years* before his release!

(Adapted from Christian History magazine, Volume 5, Number 3, and Hero Tales, Volume 2: A Family Treasury of True Stories From the Lives of Christian Heroes *by Dave and Neta Jackson.)*

Discussion Starter

Ask:
- **What do you think about John Bunyan?**
- **Would you have chosen to stay in prison if you were him? Why or why not?**

Sidelight

While in prison, John Bunyan completed part of his most famous book, *Pilgrim's Progress.*

Ask volunteers to talk about times when they stood up for something or followed their convictions even though it wasn't necessarily the popular thing to do. Begin the sharing time with your own story.

Give each student a sheet of paper and a pen or pencil. Say: **Compromise is an important part of society. And compromise isn't always bad. When you buy a car, you and the seller need to compromise to find a price that's acceptable to both of you. But there are some things that can't be compromised because they're firm truths. For example, forgiveness of sins is found only in Jesus Christ. No matter how much we want or even believe forgiveness to be found elsewhere, it isn't. On your sheet of paper, make a list of convictions you have that you aren't willing to compromise. They can be spiritual or earthly convictions.**

Ask two volunteers to each share one thing from their lists. After each volunteer has shared, ask the person:
- **Why do you hold to that conviction?**
- *What* **would you be willing to sacrifice for it?**

Ask a volunteer to read 1 Corinthians 15:1-2 aloud to the group. Then have teenagers form pairs to share their convictions, to explain *why* they hold each conviction, and to explain *what* they'd be willing to sacrifice for their convictions.

When pairs are finished, pray for the group, asking God to help everyone stand strong in their convictions.

Courage

Mary Slessor (1848–1915)

Read the following true story aloud to your students, or ask a student to read it aloud.

When Mary Slessor was a teenager, she volunteered to help organize a mission in the slums of Scotland. Despite Mary's genuine and caring efforts, many of the people the mission was designed to help opposed the work because they felt it avoided the "real" needs of the community such as improving salaries and working conditions.

On the way to one mission service, Mary found herself surrounded by a gang that was fed up with the lack of "real" help the mission had given. The leader of the gang began swinging a weight hooked to a cord at Mary's head. The weight came closer and closer to her until it brushed against her face. But Mary stood her ground. She remained completely still, looking ahead with courage and determination. Just as the weight was about to hit Mary with force, the gang leader stopped swinging it. He was amazed that a young church girl could show such courage. Maybe because Mary had endured terrible abuse at the hand of her father as a young girl, she had the strength to stand up to the intimidation of the gang.

Sidelight

Mary Slessor made the final decision to go to Africa when she heard that David Livingstone, the famous missionary doctor in Africa, had died.

At the mission, Mary learned to care for the outcast, the sick, and the poor. Her desire to serve God by loving others grew stronger as she reached out to hurting people and faced the challenges of working a mission in the slums of Scotland. As her compassion, wisdom, and strength grew, Mary felt God call her to reach out to people who were not her own. So she left her home in Scotland and went to serve the people of Africa.

As she traveled to and through Africa, the courageous young woman had to come to terms with the fact that even she had fears. Mary had once refused to cross a field because there was a cow standing in it. Mary was also terrified of crowds and public speaking. Once when speaking at a mission meeting, she stopped and asked all the men to get out of sight before she would continue. While traveling by canoe, Mary would lie in the bottom of the boat in terror or sing loudly to endure the voyage.

Despite her fears, Mary Slessor became an advocate for the women of Africa and stood up against some cruel practices of the Okoyong people. For example, local customs demanded that a mother of twins be put to death, along with her twin children. Mary saved the lives of hundreds of mothers and their twins.

One evening, Mary heard the screams of an Okoyong woman tied to stakes on the ground. A man was preparing to scald her with boiling oil because the woman had given food to a starving slave man while her husband was away. The Okoyong laws demanded that the woman be punished for her offense. Mary ran to the screaming woman and put herself between the woman and the man holding the oil. The man danced around Mary, threatening to pour the oil. Despite the boiling oil and the size of the man, Mary stood her ground. The man backed down, and the woman was saved!

Mary saved countless other lives, and she worked to end fighting between tribes and spread the message of Christ throughout Africa. By showing the courage to face her fears, Mary Slessor brought real and lasting change to African society and spirituality.

(Adapted from More Than Conquerors: Portraits of Believers From All Walks of Life, *edited by John Woodbridge.)*

Discussion Starter

Provide a medium for artistic expression for your teenagers. The more complex the medium, the longer the activity will last (and the higher the interest level of the students). For example, if you have just a few minutes, provide students with markers and paper. If you have more time, give students self-hardening clay. Other possible mediums of expression include colored pencils, crayons, watercolors, oil paints, collage supplies, and papier-mâché.

Say: **Use your supplies to express your feelings about fear. You could create a picture or a symbol that demonstrates an actual fear you have or a picture or symbol that demonstrates what fear is like to you.**

Give teenagers enough time to work on their expressions, then give volunteers an opportunity to discuss what they created.

Mary Slessor said she was frightened into becoming a Christian by an elderly neighbor woman. The woman would hold Mary's hand to a fire and tell Mary that if she didn't repent, her soul would "burn in the lowin' bleezin' fire for ever and ever." Mary vowed to never use such tactics with others.

Have students form pairs and discuss these questions:

• **Explain your feelings about fear.**

• **What are you afraid of?**

• **How are your fears like Mary Slessor's? How are they different?**

• **Read Psalm 118:6-14. How does this verse apply to fear?**

Have teenagers either adjust their expressions of fear to demonstrate a picture of courage or create new artworks to express what courage is like. Have volunteers share their new expressions.

Say: **We all have fears just as Mary Slessor did. But just as Mary faced her fears, with God's help we can face our fears. With your partner, pray for God's help regarding your fears.**

Empathy
Karl F.A. Gützlaff (1803–1851)

Read the following true story aloud to your students, or ask a student to read it aloud.

As a teenager, Karl Gützlaff was very patriotic and a bit of a romantic. In 1820, he wrote a poem praising King Frederick William III of Prussia. Amazingly, the poem eventually reached the king, who was so moved by the words that he ordered a search for the seventeen-year-old writer.

Gützlaff was a dreamer and obviously could write poetry, but he didn't have any money. He had to drop out of school and go to work. The king's officials found Gützlaff working in a shop that made women's clothing. The officials brought the surprised teenager before the Prussian king.

After talking with Gützlaff, the king ordered a scholarship for the young man to continue his studies, which Gützlaff used to prepare for missionary service. Perhaps this humble beginning helped Gützlaff treat others with the humility and empathy that made him so effective in his future role.

Gützlaff began his missionary work in Indonesia, where he learned Chinese, lived among Chinese people, and even took a Chinese name. When he felt that he was prepared enough to be effective, Gützlaff boarded a junk and headed for China. As a missionary in China, Gützlaff was able to make headway because he demonstrated that he identified with the Chinese people. Gützlaff claimed Chinese nationality, spoke fluent Chinese, wore Chinese clothes, and *lived* a Chinese lifestyle. To show their respect and appreciation for Gützlaff, the Chinese people recognized Gützlaff as a descendant of a man from China who had left the country years before.

Gützlaff's attitude and appearance enabled him to make inroads into areas of China that he otherwise would have been excluded from. Gützlaff gave many

Sidelight

Karl Gützlaff's work was not without problems. Some of the workers Gützlaff sent out with Bibles and traveling money returned with journals of journeys they had not made. Some workers even sold their Bibles back to Gützlaff's printer, who then sold the Bibles back to Gützlaff.

Chinese people their first taste of Christian literature and their first experience with Western medicine. Gützlaff's empathetic methods were utilized by the missionaries who followed, including the famous Hudson Taylor. Gützlaff's empathetic and humble attitude made him an important father of missionary work in China and the world.

(Adapted from Ambassadors for Christ: Distinguished Representatives of the Message Throughout the World, *edited by John D. Woodbridge.)*

Discussion Starter

Ask:

• **Why do you think Karl Gützlaff's dress and lifestyle were so important in his work?**

• **The story suggests that Gützlaff's beginnings shaped his later attitudes. Do you think that's true? Explain.**

• **Have you ever met a person who really understood or accepted you? How did you know you were understood or accepted?**

Sidelight

In 1844, Karl Gützlaff started the Chinese Union. The union sent Chinese workers to spread God's Word in interior China. The Chinese Union died out, but Gützlaff's efforts paved the way for Hudson Taylor's China Inland Mission. Taylor's mission became one of the largest Protestant organizations in China.

Have teenagers form three groups. Give each group a sheet of paper and a pen or pencil. Say: **Imagine that each group is a team of computer software salespeople. Your team is trying to sell a wonderful new program that allows a person to control just about everything in his or her house just by speaking. The first group is trying to sell the software to a seventy-five-year-old woman. The second group is trying to sell the software to a sixteen-year-old guy. And the third group is selling the software to a forty-year-old woman. With your group, come up with a marketing strategy for the software. In your strategy, include the obstacles you would have to overcome as well as the opportunities you see.**

After several minutes, have each group present its strategy. Then read 1 Corinthians 9:19-23 aloud. Ask:

• **How did Karl Gützlaff demonstrate this verse?**

• **How did your understanding of the person for whom you made the marketing strategy determine the way you planned on communicating?**

• **Why is it important to understand and empathize with a person in** order to communicate with him or her?

• How does empathy help us reach out to others?

• What part does empathy play in the passage I read from 1 Corinthians?

• What part does empathy play in telling others about Jesus?

Endurance

Billy Graham (born 1918)

Read the following true story aloud to your students, or ask a student to read it aloud.

When he was sixteen years old, Billy Graham became a Christian at a revival meeting led by traveling evangelist Mordecai Ham. For the next six decades, Billy Graham never turned back.

While Graham went to Bible college, he believed he wasn't a very good preacher, and he really didn't have much desire to preach. "I had one passion," he explained, "and that was to win souls." For approximately the next sixty years, Billy Graham did just that.

Sidelight

Billy Graham has had opportunities to advise several presidents of the United States. Richard Nixon was one of Graham's close friends. Graham didn't support Nixon's actions, but he did remain a friend to Nixon during the Watergate scandal.

In 1945, Billy Graham became Youth for Christ's first full-time evangelist. He made the message of the gospel relevant and alive to the young people he worked with, and many young people became Christians.

In 1949, Billy Graham became famous when he led a crusade in Los Angeles. The event was supposed to last three weeks. But people continued to fill the tent beyond capacity, and the crusade went for more than eight weeks. Thousands of people became Christians.

Despite the fame, opportunities for wealth, and influence Graham found, he didn't waver from his calling. While other preachers and evangelists became trapped in greed and hunger for power, Graham remained true to himself and true to God.

In 1974, Billy Graham preached to more than 2.7 million people in Seoul, South Korea, at one event! By 1987, Billy Graham had preached in almost every country in the world and had reached innumerable people through television, radio, and film.

He wrote various best-selling inspirational books, including *Angels: God's Secret Agents, Death and the Life After,* and *Just as I Am: The Autobiography of Billy Graham.* Billy Graham continued living in integrity over the years and continued to fulfill his calling and purpose of preaching the gospel to others.

(Adapted from Great Leaders of the Christian Church, *edited by John D. Woodbridge, and the "Billy Graham Evangelistic Association" Web site [www.billygraham.org].)*

Discussion Starter

Say: **I'd like everyone to stand on your toes for the next few minutes. Keep standing on your toes as long as you can during our discussion. If you must relax, you can, but try not to.**

Read Hebrews 12:1-3 aloud. Ask:

- **What is "the race marked out for us" that the author of Hebrews wrote about?**

- **What types of things make you lose heart in your relationship with God?**

- **How do you think Billy Graham continued in his relationship with God and in his call for all those years?**

- **What do you think of Billy Graham?**

- **How can we follow his example of endurance?**

If you have students who are still on their toes, tell them they can sit down. Then ask:

- **Why were you or weren't you able to endure standing on your toes?**

• What beliefs, actions, or things in your life will endure until you're eighty?

• What can we do right now to make sure we'll endure in our faith in the future?

Say: **Billy Graham endured as an evangelist because he lived with integrity and was faithful to God's call. No matter what spiritual knowledge you have, you can't make it without God's help. But with God's help, you can change lives and you can endure. Who knows? With God's help you may even become the next Billy Graham.**

Faith

Augustine of Hippo (354–430)

Read the following true story aloud to your students, or ask a student to read it aloud.

In his book *Confessions,* Augustine of Hippo claims that from the time he was sixteen years old, he never passed up an opportunity to sin in some way. As Augustine approached twenty, he was immersed in a sinful lifestyle. He drank, and he was sexually promiscuous. He even had a lover with whom he fathered a son.

Augustine's choices, of course, didn't lead to peace. So he turned to various philosophies and religions that promised to bring meaning while allowing him to continue in his sinful lifestyle.

The sins and philosophies Augustine looked to for happiness made him miserable. So he continued his search. Augustine and his friend, Alypius, would read the books of great philosophers while discussing and searching for truth. One day while the two men were reading Paul's letters in the Bible, Augustine came to a conclusion. "I'm certain the path to man's salvation is found only in Christ and the Holy Scriptures," he confessed.

"Then why not become a Christian?" replied Alypius. "I know," Alypius continued, "a man of your passions was not meant for a life of chastity."

"Do not mock me," retorted Augustine. "I am firmly caught in the toil of sexual pleasure, a slave to my own lust."

The two men walked out to a garden beside their home, taking Paul's letters with them. Augustine sat beneath a fig tree and began to cry. "Is there any vile thing I have not done?" he thought, tears streaming down his face.

As he was crying, Augustine heard a child singing a song. "Take up, read! Take up, read!" sang the child. So Augustine picked up the Scriptures and read

Sidelight

In confronting the ideas of Pelagius (a British monk who denied the concept of original sin), Augustine helped shape the early church's understanding of sin. Augustine argued that three major stages of sin exist. The first was before the Fall, when Adam was not able to sin. The second is after the Fall, when humans are not able to not sin. And the third is in heaven, where humans are not able to sin.

Romans 13:13-14: "not in orgies and drunkenness, not in sexual im-morality and debauchery, not in dissension and jealousy. Rather, clothe yourselves with the Lord Jesus Christ, and do not think about how to gratify the desires of the sinful nature."

Augustine finally understood what faith in Jesus was about. He came to see that faith meant letting go of what he thought he wanted and holding on to the beautiful freedom God offered. "Alypius," Augustine said, "it is done. I am a Christian."

From that day on, Augustine's life began to change. He was bap-tized, and he began to take fatherly responsibility and care for his son. Augustine studied Scripture and even became the bishop of Hippo. He helped strengthen many important Christian doctrines that were chal-lenged during his day, and he still is considered one of the great fathers of the Christian Church.

(Adapted from The Hidden Price of Greatness *by Ray Beeson and Ranelda Mack Hunsicker and* Great Leaders of the Christian Church, *edited by John D. Woodbridge.)*

Discussion Starter

Ask:

• **What intellectual barriers do you have to the Christian faith?** (Try to avoid answering everyone's difficulties and focus on hearing what the teenagers say. Make a mental note of the questions you hear, and address those questions in future conversations and devotions.)

• **Why do you think reading a Scripture passage about giving up sin pushed Augustine over the line to become a Christian?**

Say: **We all struggle at times with our faith. Sometimes the struggles are serious, such as trying to figure out if God exists. Sometimes the struggles are less serious, such as figuring out the best way to express worship. The fact that you're here demonstrates that you've made it through a struggle.**

We're going to encourage each other through our struggles by sharing our own personal stories of faith. I'd like volunteers to take turns standing in front of the group and sharing about the times Christianity just clicked for them as it did for Augustine. If you can't think of or would rather not share about such a time, you can share an experience or an insight that

Sidelight

Augustine taught that faith is not inferior to rea-son. He expressed the fa-mous phrase "Credo ut inelligam," which means "I believe in order that I may know."

has helped you hold on to your faith in times of struggle.

Give each teenager an opportunity to share. Then read aloud Hebrews 11:1. Ask:

- **What is faith to you?**
- **What is faith according to the passage I just read?**
- **How do these stories make you feel about your faith?**
- **How can each of us strengthen our own faith?**

Spend time in group prayer, asking God to help your teenagers through the struggles of their faith. Encourage youth to silently lift those struggles up in prayer. Then ask:

- **Does anyone want to know more about what it means to be a Christian?**

Dismiss the rest of the group. Then take students who want to know what it means to be a Christian through the following Scriptures:

1. Romans 3:23
2. Romans 6:23
3. Romans 5:8
4. Romans 10:9-10.

Give students who aren't Christians an opportunity to make a commitment to Jesus. Then close the devotion by praying for (or with) each student.

Faithfulness

Polycarp (70–155)

Read the following true story aloud to your students, or ask a student to read it aloud.

When the Christian Church was still very young, Polycarp gained a reputation as a man who stood up for truth and for Christ. Less than eighty years after Jesus died, Polycarp was named the bishop of Smyrna—the man who would have to lead the Christians of the city through the Roman persecution. Despite the hatred and opposition Polycarp faced for leading the Church and spreading the gospel, he remained faithful to the call God had given him. The citizens of Smyrna couldn't bear to hear the bold teachings and challenges of Polycarp's Christianity. So they pushed for his arrest.

Three days before he was arrested, Polycarp had a vision. While praying for the early church, he saw his pillow burst into flames. Polycarp immediately realized that God had given him a picture of his future, and he told his friends he would be burned alive for the sake of the gospel.

When the authorities arrived to arrest Polycarp, Polycarp met the men, served them a meal, and willingly went with them to face the proconsul—the Roman governor. The proconsul interrogated and threatened Polycarp because Christianity was seen as a heretical and godless cult by the Romans. Christians were seen as atheists because they didn't believe in the Roman gods.

"Swear by the genius of Caesar," demanded the proconsul, "Repent (and) say 'Away with the atheists.' "

"Away with the atheists," Polycarp declared after waving his hands at the crowd.

"Swear, and I will release you; curse the Christ," returned the proconsul.

"Eighty-six years I served him, and he has done me no wrong; how can I blaspheme my king who has saved me?" answered Polycarp.

"I have wild beasts; if you do not repent, I will throw you to them," warned the proconsul.

"Send them," retorted Polycarp. "For repentance from better to worse is not a change permitted to us."

"I will make you be consumed by fire if you don't repent," answered the proconsul.

"You threaten the fire that burns for an hour and in a little while is quenched; for you know not of the fire of judgment to come, and the fire of the eternal punishment reserved for the ungodly. But why do you delay? Bring what you will," answered Polycarp.

The crowd could no longer stand to hear Polycarp's words. His assertion that *they* were headed for hell nearly caused a riot. So they demanded that the proconsul end the interrogation and that Polycarp be killed.

The angry mob collected wood and prepared to nail him to a stake. Polycarp assured the crowd that nails weren't necessary and that God would help him to stay in the burning wood without moving. The mob lit the fire and burned Polycarp. To make certain that he would die, the mob had an executioner stab Polycarp with a dagger. That day, Polycarp died a faithful father and martyr of the Christian Church.

(Adapted from Christian History magazine, Volume 9, Number 3.)

Sidelight

While Polycarp's martyrdom is a historical fact, there are some unbelievable claims in the retelling of the event. The Christians in Smyrna wrote an account of Polycarp's death shortly after he was martyred. They claimed that Polycarp's body wouldn't be consumed by the fire, so the people had an executioner stab Polycarp with a dagger. When Polycarp was stabbed, a dove came out of him, along with so much blood that the fire was put out.

Discussion Starter

Have teenagers form trios to read Matthew 26:31-35; 69-75 aloud. After trios are finished reading, have them discuss these questions:

• **Why do you think Polycarp was able to remain faithful and Peter wasn't?**

• **Do you identify more with Polycarp or Peter?**

Have students form pairs. Have each person share with a partner what unfaithfulness to Jesus is like in his or her life or describe a time when he or she was unfaithful. Consider sharing first to model appropriate responses and stories. For example, you might tell students about a time you failed to share your faith with someone, or a time you lied or cheated.

Say: **Thank you for your honesty. We all have been unfaithful to Jesus in one way or another. But even if we're unfaithful, Jesus is always** faithful to us. Peter denied Jesus publicly, but Peter was given another chance. Peter learned from his unfaithfulness. He became such a faithful follower of Christ that he was later martyred for his faith.

Ask:

• **Do you think you would follow Peter's and Polycarp's example if you were being persecuted to the point of death? Explain.**

• **Are you a faithful follower of Christ? Explain.**

Have students form a circle. Have each person in the circle share what faithfulness to Jesus means to him or her and a time when the person was faithful. After everyone has shared, say: **May you go and faithfully do likewise. Amen.**

Sidelight

Born in 70, Polycarp knew people who had been eyewitnesses of Jesus' time on earth. Some historians believe Polycarp knew the apostle John.

Focus

George Frideric Handel (1685–1759)

Read the following true story aloud to your students, or ask a student to read it aloud.

George Handel's father didn't want his son to bother with music. The elder Handel was a surgeon who worked in the court of a royal household, and he wanted his son to become a lawyer. But young George had a passion for music. While young Handel's father worked, the boy would sneak away and play the palace instruments.

Handel was quite talented, and at the age of nine he was asked to play the organ at a royal church service. Handel's playing was so brilliant, a duke talked Handel's father into allowing young George to take lessons. George became an amazing musician and composer.

More than anything else, Handel loved to set Scripture to music. He would pour his soul into the pieces and work ceaselessly until he felt they were perfect. While composing *Messiah,* Handel worked in his house without leaving for twenty-four straight days! His servant brought him trays of food, but Handel was so focused that he ate only small bites now and then. He did almost nothing except study the Bible and compose music. When Handel was finally finished and he felt that he had perfected the piece, he went to his servant with tears in his eyes and exclaimed, "I did think I did see all Heaven before me, and the great God himself!"

Sidelight

Eight years before he died, Handel became blind. Despite the difficulty, he continued conducting music.

(Adapted from the In Touch Ministries Web site [www.intouch.org/INTOUCH/portraits/george_frideric_handel.html].)

Discussion Starter

Have teenagers form pairs, and give each pair a Bible. Say: **Choose one person in your pair to be the Memorizer and the other person to be the Distracter. The Memorizer has two minutes to commit Philippians 3:12-14 to memory. The Distracter should do everything in his or her power to stop** the Memorizer without touching him or her. Get ready to begin.

Have pairs begin, and let them know when two minutes are up. Then have pairs reverse the roles and repeat the exercise. Ask:

- **How many of you were able to memorize the passage?**
- **What part did the distractions play in your success?**
- **What would it take for you to memorize the passage?**
- **How do you keep your focus when you want to successfully complete something?**
- **Why do you think Handel was able to have such intense focus as he composed *Messiah*?**
- **Have you ever experienced a time when you were focused? Explain.**

Have a volunteer read Philippians 3:12-14 aloud. Say: **One of the reasons Paul accomplished so much was that he had incredible focus. His whole life was completely focused on Christ. Before you have that kind of focus, you have to decide if the object of your focus is worth the price of your concentration and devotion. I'm going to play "The Hallelujah Chorus." This famous piece of music is part of Handel's *Messiah*. While the music is playing, I'd like you to think about what you're going to focus your life on and how you're going to do it.**

Play Handel's "Hallelujah Chorus." When the piece is over, give students an opportunity to share what they decided.

Foresight

Jim Elliot (1927–1956)

Read the following true story aloud to your students, or ask a student to read it aloud.

In the jungles of the Amazon lived a tribe of people called the Huaorani. The Huaorani had never heard the truth of the gospel until a group of five young missionaries set out to share the good news of Jesus. Jim Elliot, Nate Saint, Ed McCully, Pete Fleming, and Roger Youderian knew that the Huaorani would be difficult to reach. The people were known for killing every outsider who dared to cross their path. Employees of the oil companies and other foreigners that encroached on the Huaorani territory were ambushed at their own camps or speared to death when they ventured into the jungle.

Despite the reputation of the Huaorani, the group of missionaries determined to share God's Word with the tribe. The men began by flying over the tribe in Nate Saint's plane and dropping gifts to the people. The Huaorani accepted the gifts and sent gifts in return. One bold Huaorani even approached the missionaries and asked for a ride in Nate's plane. The missionaries gladly obliged.

The men seemed to be making tremendous progress. So they decided to make direct contact with the Huaorani. Gikita, one of the older Huaorani, remembered previous negative encounters with white men. He knew that white men could be vicious and often took what didn't belong to them. He also had been given a false report that the missionaries had attacked a few of the Huaorani people. So Gikita led a group of Huaorani warriors to meet the missionaries.

The missionaries were carrying guns, but they had agreed beforehand that they wouldn't attack in self-defense the people they were called to reach—even if it meant death. The missionaries believed that sharing the gospel was more important than their own lives, and they knew a show of force would ruin their chances of telling the people about Jesus. So as Gikita and the band of warriors began their attack on the missionaries, the men didn't fight back.

The spears whistled through the air. "We just came to meet you.

We aren't going to hurt you. Why are you killing us?" one of the missionaries cried in broken Huao. One of the Huaorani listened to the plea, then thrust his spear into the missionary's body. Even though they had more than enough firepower to overcome and overwhelm the Huaorani, all five of the missionaries were killed. None of the Huaorani were seriously injured.

Three years after the men were murdered, Jim Elliot's wife, Elisabeth, and Nate Saint's sister, Rachel, continued the work their loved ones had begun. The women boldly approached the tribe who had recently killed their relatives. Surprisingly, the women were accepted by the Huaorani. And in time, many of the people who had killed their family members came to believe in Jesus.

Gikita and the other Huaorani people later explained that the only reason they allowed the women to interact with the tribe was the fact that they knew the missionary men could have fought back but chose not to. The choice the men made to die rather than fight opened the door for the tribe to find salvation.

(Adapted from Martyrs: Contemporary Writers on Modern Lives of Faith, *edited by Susan Bergman, and* More Than Conquerors: Portraits of Believers From All Walks of Life, *edited by John Woodbridge.)*

Discussion Starter

Before your meeting, fill two cups one-fourth full with clear vinegar and two cups one-fourth full with water. Have teenagers form two groups. Set one cup of vinegar and one cup of water in front of each group. Set baking soda and a spoon in front of each group. Direct each group to put a spoonful of baking soda in each of the cups. Make sure you have towels nearby, because the vinegar may bubble over.

Ask:

• **How many of you were expecting the results you had with each cup?**

• **If you weren't expecting those results, what did you think when the one cup started bubbling?**

Say: **While some of you may have known what was going to happen, your group just demonstrated the effects of our actions as Christians. Sometimes when we choose to live for God, there is no visible or**

Sidelight

When he was twenty-two, Jim Elliot wrote the famous words, "He is no fool who gives what he cannot keep to gain what he cannot lose."

long-term change that happens in those around us. But sometimes our actions—even very simple ones—can lead to a chain reaction in someone's life.

The missionaries had no way of knowing their refusal to fight would open up an opportunity for the Huaorani to believe in Jesus. But they did have the foresight to understand that making a choice to fight could hinder future missionary efforts. Whether you like it or not, people are watching you, and it's essential that you live your life thinking about how it will affect them. You never know when God will bring you back into a person's life or how your actions will come back to you in the future. Therefore, I leave you with this challenge:

Read Colossians 3:17 aloud to your group.

Forgiveness

Corrie ten Boom (1892–1983)

Read the following true story aloud to your students, or ask a student to read it aloud.

Corrie ten Boom was a very ordinary Dutch woman. That is, until the Nazis occupied the Netherlands during World War II. Corrie and her family refused to ignore the atrocities that were taking place against their Jewish neighbors. So they opened their home to hide Jewish families from the German Gestapo—the secret police.

A fellow Dutchman turned the ten Booms in to the Gestapo. As a result, Corrie and her sister were taken to Ravensbruck—a women's death camp operated by the Nazis. Their father was taken to prison, where he died. At Ravensbruck, Corrie and her sister, Betsy, endured forced labor, rat-infested and unheated barracks, malnutrition, disease, and physical abuse. Corrie lost her sister to the Nazi camp.

Despite the awful conditions at Ravensbruck, Corrie led Bible studies and prayer meetings. She even shared scarce food and much-needed medical supplies with the other prisoners. Then miraculously, Corrie was released from Ravensbruck on a clerical error—one week before the rest of the women in her age group were exterminated.

After the war ended, Corrie went back to Ravensbruck to share the gospel with the people responsible for her pain and horror. She spoke of God's forgiveness, encouraging the people to accept God's gift. After she had finished speaking at one meeting, she found herself face to face with one of the guards from Ravensbruck. The man had been one of the most despicable and cruel people she had encountered in the camp. He extended his hand to Corrie, seeking the forgiveness she talked about and offered.

"It could not have been many seconds that he stood there," Corrie recalled. "But to me it seemed hours as I wrestled with the most difficult thing I ever had to do." While wrestling with her pain and remembering the loss of her sister, she prayed. Then Corrie forced her hand into the hand of the guard. And Jesus gave her the strength to forgive. She began to feel overwhelmed with joy and freedom as she said, "I do forgive you, brother. With all my heart."

(Adapted from More Than Conquerors: Portraits of Believers From All Walks of Life, *edited by John Woodbridge, and* Hero Tales, Volume 2: A Family Treasury of True Stories From the Lives of Christian Heroes, *by Dave and Neta Jackson.)*

Discussion Starter

Give each student an object that's cumbersome or uncomfortable to hold. For example, you might have students hold books out in front of themselves, or you could have teenagers hold chairs above their heads. While students are holding the objects, ask:

• **Have you ever had a difficult time extending forgiveness to a person who hurt you? Explain.**

• **What does it mean to forgive?**

• **How do you forgive someone if you're still angry at the person?**

• **What does it feel like to finally forgive a person you've been angry at?**

Read Colossians 3:12-14 aloud. Allow teenagers to set down the objects they're holding. Then say: **Unforgiveness hurts and hinders the person who won't forgive more than the**

Sidelight

After her experience in Ravensbruck, Corrie ten Boom shared her story to inspire millions of people. She recorded her story in the book *The Hiding Place* and traveled to more than sixty-four countries in her thirty-three years of public ministry.

person who isn't forgiven. Unforgiveness is much like the object you were holding up. The longer you hold on to it, the greater a burden it becomes. When you forgive someone, you aren't saying that what the person did was OK. You are saying that you'll let go of your hate, your bitterness, and your right to revenge. You're choosing to love someone who may not even deserve your love. This kind of forgiveness is difficult to do, but we must remember that God has extended this kind of forgiveness to us.

I'm going to give you three minutes of complete silence. During that time, I'd like you to ask God to bring to mind people you need to forgive. Then if possible, choose to forgive those people. After you've forgiven someone, pray for him or her, and ask God to heal your heart.

Generosity
Amanda Smith (1837–1915)

Read the following true story aloud to your students, or ask a student to read it aloud.

Amanda Smith's father worked day and night until he had enough money to buy his family out of slavery. The family moved to Pennsylvania, where Amanda could work, play, and live a free woman. Enjoying her new freedom, Amanda was married at the age of seventeen. Unfortunately, the marriage ended when her husband went to fight in the Civil War and was killed. So Amanda married again and had a daughter named Maizie. But when Amanda was thirty-two years old, her second husband died. So Amanda was forced to support herself and Maizie by doing washing and ironing for other people.

Amanda and Maizie endured overwhelming poverty. Most of the money Amanda brought in went to meet basic necessities. She had to scrap and save for a long time just to buy Maizie shoes. After much hard work, Amanda had managed to store away two dollars—just enough money to buy Maizie a new pair of shoes! Amanda was excited and relieved to have the opportunity to buy shoes for Maizie, and she planned to do it soon after she attended a big-tent revival.

Sidelight

Amanda Smith became a well-known and effective missionary and traveling evangelist. After her experience with the Indian missionary, Amanda served in England and India.

A missionary had come to the meeting to talk about India and the desperate need for resources to share the good news of Jesus with the people of India. Amanda couldn't bear to hear of the many people who didn't know Jesus, and she wanted to help. Amanda felt God tell her to give the two dollars to the missionary. It was all the money Amanda had, and she really wanted to buy Maizie a new pair of shoes. But Amanda trusted God and gave the money to the missionary.

Instead of going to buy shoes after the meeting, Amanda and Maizie went over to a friend's house for dinner. As usual, all the plates had been turned upside down to keep the dust off. After giving thanks, Amanda turned over her plate to start the meal. She was surprised to find three dollars sitting under her plate—one more dollar than she needed for Maizie's new shoes.

(Adapted from Hero Tales, Volume 2: A Family Treasury of True Stories From the Lives of Christian Heroes *by Dave and Neta Jackson.)*

Discussion Starter

Have students form groups of four. Say: **Imagine that while I was walking to our meeting, I found a winning lottery ticket. If I told your group you could have $4 million as long as you spend the money on charity, what would your group do with the money?**

Give groups about three minutes to decide what they would do with the money, and allow each group to share its plan. Then ask:

• **What are you doing right now for the causes you mentioned?**

• **Why do people think they need to have an abundance of money before they can be generous?**

Have groups read Luke 21:1-4. Ask:

• **What does this passage teach us about generosity?**

• **Does God always award generosity as with Amanda Smith? Explain.**

• **Does God award generosity in other ways? Explain.**

Say: **God doesn't care about the size or greatness of the gifts we give. God cares about the attitudes behind those gifts. God doesn't always return or increase the money and gifts we give away. But God does use them. God uses our gifts to help others and to bring joy to our hearts. No matter how much you have, you can be generous with it. And God will bless your generosity.**

Grace

John Newton (1725–1807)

Read the following true story aloud to your students, or ask a student to read it aloud.

When he was eleven years old, John Newton left school to begin a life at sea. He worked on his father's ship, then worked on various other vessels, including ships that collected slaves off the west African coast. As Newton gained experience as a sailor, he eventually became captain of his own slave ship. The slave trade was a wicked and cruel business, and the people who worked the ships became wicked and cruel themselves. Newton was no exception. His heart quickly hardened as he sold human beings for profit. Newton clearly had no desire for or interest in God.

Then on March 10, 1748, while returning to England from Africa, Newton's ship ran into heavy storms. Newton and his crew were terrified—certain they would die at sea. The experience shattered the hardness of Newton's heart. He began to think about his life and to realize the certainty of his death.

Newton turned to the book *Imitation of Christ* to find relief and guidance. The book helped Newton understand his need for Jesus. And Newton was in desperate need. After all, he had made a living out of stripping people from their families and villages and selling them to the highest bidder. But through God's grace, the hard and wicked man turned to Christ and found *complete* forgiveness.

After becoming a Christian, Newton tried to justify his work by improving conditions on the slave ships. He even held worship services for his crew. But Newton's efforts couldn't conceal the horrors of the slave trade. Newton had no choice but to quit his job as captain and become a clerk in England.

While in England, Newton felt that God wanted him to become a pastor. He began his studies and at the age of thirty-nine took a position in his first church. He spoke out strongly against the slave trade

Sidelight

John Newton worked together with his friend, William Cowper, to create the *Olney Hymns* hymnal. Newton wrote 282 of the 349 hymns it contained.

and became a respected pastor and hymn writer. His most famous hymn of all clearly comes from his own experience of being transformed from a wicked slave-trade captain to an Anglican pastor—it's called "Amazing Grace."

(Adapted from 101 Hymn Stories *by Kenneth W. Osbeck.)*

Discussion Starter

Before this devotion, make one photocopy of the "Candy Bar Instructions" handout (p. 45) for each student in your group.

Give each person one copy of the handout and one candy bar. Give students enough time to get through all the directions on the handout. If students give you an unopened candy bar, give them two candy bars in return. Then say: **This exercise demonstrates what sin is like. We rush into situations without checking God's direction, and we lose out on God's blessing. If you rushed into this handout without reading the instructions, you missed out on a double portion.**

Sidelight

Shortly before his death, John Newton is quoted as saying, "My memory is nearly gone, but I remember two things: That I am a great sinner and that Christ is a great Savior!"

Now I'm going to demonstrate what grace is all about. Read 1 Timothy 1:12-17 aloud. Then say: **Give me your open wrapper *or* the discarded half of your candy bar, and I'll give you two candy bars in return.** Give two candy bars to each student who gives you his or her wrapper or discarded candy bar. Say: **There isn't a thing you can do about your sin except to turn to God. And when you turn to God for forgiveness, God gives it to you for free. All you need to do is give Jesus the trash and shambles of your life.**

Candy Bar Instructions

Read this handout, and then follow the instructions.

1. Ask someone what his or her favorite candy bar is. Write his or her answer here.

2. Give at least two different people nicknames from the names of candy bars. For example, you could call someone who laughs "Snickers." Tell the people their nicknames, then have them initial here.

3. Open your candy bar.

4. Break your candy bar in half. Throw half of your candy bar in the trash.

5. Eat the other half of your candy bar.

6. Write a short poem that uses the names of at least three different candy bars.

7. Ignore the first six directions on this handout.

8. Take your unopened candy bar to the leader, and exchange it for two candy bars.

9. Talk quietly with your friends while you wait for further instructions.

Honesty

Wang Ming-tao (1900–1991)

Read the following true story aloud to your students, or ask a student to read it aloud.

Wang Ming-tao didn't want to be in full-time ministry. Pastors in China received poor salaries, and they weren't respected. But in 1918, Wang came down with a sickness that almost took his life. While he was ill, he promised God he would go into ministry if he survived the illness. Wang survived, and he kept his promise.

Wang started a Christian church that saw many changes and faced many difficulties in China. During the Sino-Japanese war from 1937 to 1945, Peking fell under Japanese control. The Japanese-led Chinese Christian Federation of North China pressured Wang to join its ranks. Wang refused because of theological differences. He made this decision knowing that he would probably be killed for his stand. In fact, Wang kept a coffin in his house in preparation for the federation's response. Miraculously, the federation never took action against Wang.

In 1949, the communists came to power in China. The communist government heavily persecuted the Chinese Christian church. Strict rules were imposed on the church, and many church leaders were imprisoned. But Wang Ming-tao stood strong and continued as a leader in the Chinese church.

The communist government imprisoned Wang. While in prison, Wang faced ceaseless questioning and interrogation. He was a prominent leader of the Christian church in China, and the government knew that breaking Wang would be a severe blow to the church. So the officials pressed, persecuted, and badgered Wang until the exhausted man confessed to resisting state control of the church. In response to Wang's confession, the government released him from prison.

After his release, Wang Ming-tao regretted his decision to sign the confession. He felt that cooperation with the tactics of communist intimidation and communist ideology was a betrayal of his Lord. While he dreaded returning to the harassment and persecution of the Chinese prison, he felt he had to be completely honest and upright before

God. So Wang and his wife appeared before the government and re-voked their confessions. As they expected, they were both quickly thrown into prison for their bold honesty, and they remained there for the next twenty years.

(Adapted from Ambassadors for Christ: Distinguished Representatives of the Message Throughout the World, *edited by John D. Woodbridge.)*

Discussion Starter

Ask:

• **Do you think Wang Ming-tao made the right choice when he re-voked his confession?**

• **Would you have made the same choice?**

• **Why do you think Wang signed the confession in the first place?**

• **Think about the last lie you told. Why did you break the truth?**

Read Proverbs 29:25 aloud. Say: **Most dishonesty comes from fear-ing people more than fearing God. For example, sometimes we lie to avoid getting in trouble. Sometimes we lie to make others think highly of us. Other times we lie to get our way with people. But if we fear God, we must be honest. God's opin-ion and judgment are much more important than the opinion or judgment of any person. Wang Ming-tao's story shows us that it's never too late to be honest. Like Wang, we must be willing to face the conse-quences of truth.**

Sidelight

Wang Ming-tao was re-leased from prison in 1979 as China's Teng Hsiao-ping ushered in an era of greater tolerance for the Christian church. Wang lived and labored for Christ for twelve years after his release.

Give each student a sheet of paper, a pen or pencil, and a copy of the "Confession" handout (pp. 48-49). Say: **I'd like you to write your own confession. Unlike the confession Wang signed, your confession should be either a statement of repentance for fearing peo-ple more than God or a declaration of what you believe to be true about God. Before you begin, read Deuteronomy 10:12-22. You won't have to show your confession to anyone if you don't want to.**

After about five minutes, give students an opportunity to share their confessions with the group.

Confession

As you create your confession, you can use the Apostle's Creed and the Nicene Creed as references. Write your confession in the space provided.

The Apostle's Creed

I believe in God, the Father almighty, maker of heaven and earth.

And in Jesus Christ his only Son our Lord; who was conceived by the Holy Spirit, born of the Virgin Mary, suffered under Pontius Pilate, was crucified, dead and buried. He descended into hell. The third day he rose again from the dead. He ascended into heaven and sits at the right hand of God the Father almighty. From thence he shall come to judge the living and the dead.

I believe in the Holy Spirit, the holy Christian Church, the communion of saints, the forgiveness of sins, the resurrection of the body, and the life everlasting. Amen.

The Nicene Creed

We believe in one God, the Father, the Almighty, maker of heaven and earth, of all that is, seen and unseen.

We believe in one Lord, Jesus Christ, the only Son of God, eternally begotten of the Father, God from God, Light from Light, true God from true God, begotten, not made, of one Being with the Father. Through him all things were made. For us and for our salvation he came down from heaven: by the power of the Holy Spirit he became incarnate from the Virgin Mary, and was made man. For our sake he was crucified under Pontius Pilate; he suffered death and was buried. On the third day he rose again in accordance with the Scriptures; he ascended into heaven and is seated at the right hand of the Father. He will come again in glory to judge the living and the dead, and his kingdom will have no end.

We believe in the Holy Spirit, the Lord, the giver of life, who proceeds from the Father and the Son. With the Father and the Son he is worshipped and glorified. He has spoken through the Prophets. We believe in one holy catholic and apostolic Church. We acknowledge one baptism for the forgiveness of sins. We look for the resurrection of the dead, and the life of the world to come. Amen.

Write your confession below:

Hope
Martin Luther (1483–1546)

Read the following true story aloud to your students, or ask a student to read it aloud.

It was the worst time in Martin Luther's life. Ten years before this dark period, Luther had posted his 95 Theses listing the problems he saw with the established church. Since then, Luther's life had been in danger, and he was constantly attacked and challenged by those around him. He was emotionally and physically bankrupt, and he began suffering from periodic dizzy spells.

One night when friends arrived for dinner, Luther felt an intense buzzing in his ear. He went to lie down and called, "Water…or I'll die!" Luther was convinced he was going to die that very night. Fortunately, Luther didn't die. But he had bouts with depression and illness for the next five months. He was in pain from head to toe, and he truly felt as if Christ had abandoned him. More than once, Luther considered turning his back on God.

Sidelight

Martin Luther often became angry with members of his congregation for continuing in their sin despite his warnings and instructions. One time Luther exclaimed, "It annoys me to keep preaching to you." In 1530, Luther actually went on strike and refused to preach for a time.

On top of his own troubles, the plague had been spreading in Wittenberg, the city where Luther lived. Luther opened his home to the sick, and many of Luther's friends died. Even Luther's own son became ill.

But it was during this time of darkness that Luther wrote his most famous hymn. It is a hymn that affirms God's strength and protection, and it demonstrates that Martin Luther held on to hope even in the worst time of his life. And most important, this hymn has brought hope to countless Christians through the centuries: "A Mighty Fortress Is Our God." The third verse demonstrates the outcome of Luther's dark year:

Though devils all the world should fill,

All eager to devour us,

We tremble not, we fear no ill,

They shall not overpower us.

This world's prince may still

Scowl fierce as he will,

He can harm us none,

He's judged; the deed is done;

One little word can fell him.

(Adapted from Christian History magazine, Volume 12, Number 3, and Rick's MGV "Harmonia" Page [www.acronet.net/~robokopp/hymn/amightyf.html].)

Discussion Starter

Say: **I want you to think of a time when you lost hope. It could be your darkest hour or a time when you were simply frustrated. How did you get through the situation?** Share your own story of lost hope. Then ask for volunteers to share their stories.

After everyone has had a chance to share, have teenagers form groups of three. Say: **Imagine that a girl named Angela has just called you for help. Her older brother recently died in a car accident. Her parents have separated because of the strain of losing their son. She is barely surviving school, and she doesn't know what to do. You've already persuaded Angela to talk with your pastor the next morning. But she needs hope right now. With your group, determine what you would say to Angela.**

After about five minutes, ask each group to share its response. Explain that you often turn to God's Word for hope. Then share a passage from Scripture that gives you hope, or read Psalm 40:1-3 aloud.

Ask:

• **Can you think of any other Scriptures that give you hope?**

• **Where else do you find hope?**

Say: **As Christians, we can have hope. We know that God is always with us. God will give us the grace to get through every difficult thing. And we know that no matter what happens, we will have perfect peace and relief when God calls us home to heaven.**

Sidelight

Martin Luther was so generous that people sometimes took advantage of him. Luther and his wife, Katherine, took in a woman who claimed to be a runaway nun, only to discover that she had lied and stolen. Luther responded to such situations by saying, "God divided the hand into fingers so that money would slip through."

Industry

Charles Wesley (1707–1788)

Read the following true story aloud to your students, or ask a student to read it aloud.

Charles Wesley wrote 8,989 hymns! Some of Wesley's hymns include "Hark! The Herald Angels Sing," "O for a Thousand Tongues to Sing," and "Christ the Lord Is Risen Today." Wesley was not only an incredible composer; he was also an incredible preacher. He chose to preach *outside* church buildings, an idea that was unthinkable during his day. One sermon drew a crowd of twenty thousand people! More than once, Wesley preached to crowds of ten thousand listeners.

But Wesley wasn't born great. In fact, he was born prematurely. Greatness for Wesley came through God's direction and Wesley's hard work. As a child, Wesley's mother taught him Greek, Latin, and French for six hours every day! Wesley then spent thirteen years at Westminster School and the next nine years at Oxford. Wesley could recite memorized poems written by Virgil that took thirty minutes to recite—in Latin! It's very likely that Wesley had at least all of Ephesians 6 memorized in Greek!

Sidelight

The religious group Charles Wesley founded with his brother, John Wesley, was called both "Methodists" and "Precisianists." Fortunately, the former name stuck.

There's no doubt that God gave Wesley guidance and gifts. But Wesley put those gifts to work. His diligent study strengthened and refined the talents he was given. If Wesley hadn't worked and studied, Christianity would have missed out on some of its most-loved songs. And the denomination now known as the Methodist Church may never have been started.

(Adapted from Christian History magazine, Volume 10, Number 3.)

Discussion Starter

Give each teenager an index card and a pen or pencil. Say: **Think of one thing you're good at. For example, you may be a good swimmer, a good student, or a talented musician. Now think of how many hours on** average you devote to that talent each week. Write that number on your card and multiply it by fifty-two. Now multiply that number by the number of years you've been participating in the activity.

The number you have demonstrates how many hours you've spent on that talent or activity to reach your current skill level. Divide that number by twenty-four to see how many solid days and nights you've spent working on that skill.

Sidelight

To complete his 8,989 hymns, Charles Wesley would have had to write, on average, ten lines of verse every day for fifty years.

Give teenagers a chance to share what they've discovered. Then ask:

• **How does your current skill level compare to the level of skill you'd have if you spent twice as much time practicing?**

Say: **God has given you natural talents and abilities just as God gave to Charles Wesley. But you'll never reach your full potential in any area of your life unless you work at it. It takes hundreds of hours to become excellent at anything. Charles Wesley became a great composer and preacher because he studied and worked at it. You also can become great, but you must practice and work on the gifts God has given you.**

Next have students complete the above exercise to determine how much time they've spent on their spiritual growth. Ask:

• **How would your relationship with and understanding of God be different if you spent twice as much time working on your spiritual growth?**

Ask a volunteer to read 1 Corinthians 9:24-27 aloud. Ask:

• **What does this verse say about spiritual practice and training?**

• **How much time and practice do you think Paul put into spiritual growth?**

• **How can you follow Paul's example?**

Integrity

Sam Hill (1867–1936) and John Nicholson (1859–1946)

Read the following true story aloud to your students, or ask a student to read it aloud.

John Nicholson was a traveling paper salesman in the late 1800s. He had just finished a long day riding trains and carriages and meeting appointments, and he didn't reach his hotel until nine o'clock that evening. To his dismay, every room in the hotel was filled. The hotel manager offered one last option to Nicholson.

"We have a man with us tonight by the name of Sam Hill, a good, clean fellow," the manager said. "There's a spare bed in his room, and if you're both willing to share, you could have it." Hill and Nicholson both agreed to the arrangement.

Sam Hill rolled over to go to sleep when Nicholson explained that he needed to keep the light on a little longer to read the Bible and pray. Hill responded, "Read it aloud. I'm a Christian, too."

After Nicholson finished reading, the men talked about the need for Christian salesmen to know about each other. By early the next morning, they had decided they would start an association. The men left the hotel excited about their plans. But as time went on, both Hill and Nicholson failed to act on their commitment, and they forgot about their plans.

Eight months later, the two men had a chance meeting on a street in Beaver Dam, Wisconsin. They remembered the plans they had made together and resolved to follow through this time. Two months later, they had their first meeting. Hill, Nicholson, and one other person by the name of William Knights showed up. Despite the poor turnout, the men refused to get discouraged. They appointed themselves president, vice president, and secretary-treasurer. The men continued to meet, and the organization called the Gideons continued to grow.

As the organization developed, the Gideons decided to work to place a Bible in every hotel room in the country. Every year, the Gideons get reports of business people who in desperation open the

Bibles in their hotel rooms to find freedom and salvation in Christ. If Nicholson and Hill hadn't followed through on their commitment, millions of hotels and individuals would be without Bibles. In fact, today it's not uncommon for the Gideons to distribute more than 30 million Bibles in one year!

(Adapted from Christian History magazine, Volume 10, Number 3.)

Discussion Starter

Ask:

• **Why do you think it took a second meeting before Nicholson and Hill took action?**

• **What would have happened if Nicholson and Hill had never met again?**

Have teenagers form pairs. Say: **On their first meeting, Nicholson and Hill made an agreement they didn't keep. Tell your partner about a time when someone broke his or her word to you or didn't live up to a promise.**

After pairs have shared, ask:

• **How did you feel about the person when he or she didn't keep his or her word?**

• **Why do you think people say it's important to have integrity and to keep your word?**

• **Do you agree? Why or why not?**

Read Proverbs 11:3 aloud. Then have pairs share about times they broke their word or didn't live up to their promises. When pairs are finished, ask:

• **How did you feel when you broke your word?**

• **How do you think the other person felt about you?**

Read Proverbs 11:3 aloud again. Ask:

• **According to this verse, why is it important for you to have integrity?**

Say: **Fortunately, God gave Sam Hill and John Nicholson a second chance to stay true to their word. Perhaps the Gideons never would have come into existence if Hill and Nicholson had ignored their second chance. If you've struggled with having integrity, you have a second chance. But it's important to take the opportunity. With your partner, share one area in which you feel the Holy Spirit is guiding you to have integrity. When you're both finished sharing, pray for each other. Next time we meet, ask your partner how he or she did.**

Joy
Peter Cartwright (1785–1872)

Read the following true story aloud to your students, or ask a student to read it aloud.

Peter Cartwright became a Christian when he was fifteen years old. Then he spent fifty-three of the next fifty-five years riding the trail and bringing the gospel to families on the frontier in Kentucky, Tennessee, Indiana, Ohio, and Illinois.

It was at one of Cartwright's camp meetings in Kentucky that a woman named Mrs. Stewart was changed forever. The respected preacher stood before the crowd and preached. "The Bible says, 'Love your neighbor as yourself,' " Cartwright said. "Think about this, my friends. Would you like to be treated like a piece of property? Would you like to be bought and sold and have no freedom? Yet that is how people treat slaves. You slave owners, are you treating these slaves as you would like to be treated? Are you obeying God?"

Sidelight

Peter Cartwright moved his family to Illinois, where he met Abraham Lincoln.

The words cut to Mrs. Stewart's heart, since she was a slave owner. As others spent the week singing praises and thanking God for his gifts, Mrs. Stewart could think of nothing but the unhappy lives of her slaves. Mrs. Stewart tried to put her thoughts behind her, praying that God would fill her heart with joy. But the joy never came. Finally Mrs. Stewart fell to her knees and prayed to God, "If you will give me joy, we will give up our slaves and set them free."

Immediately, God flooded Mrs. Stewart's heart with joy—so much so that she thought she might be dreaming. Mrs. Stewart stood to her feet and proclaimed, "Thank God, he's given me joy!" After Mrs. Stewart told the camp members about her experience, many people became Christians, many Christians repented for keeping slaves, and many Christians made the decision to release their slaves.

(Adapted from Hero Tales, Volume 2: A Family Treasury of True Stories From the Lives of Christian Heroes *by Dave and Neta Jackson.)*

Discussion Starter

Ask:

• **Why couldn't Mrs. Stewart find joy until she agreed to give up her slaves?**

    • **How do our choices affect the joy we have?**

    • **What things other than our choices affect the joy we have?**

    • **How is joy different from happiness?**

Give each student a sheet of paper and a pen or pencil. Say: **On a scale of one to ten, where one is no joy at all and ten is complete joy, what is your current joy level? Write that number on your sheet of paper. Then write a list of all the circumstances, attitudes, and sins that are affecting your joy.**

Have teenagers form pairs to read John 15:9-12. Then ask:

    • **How can our joy be complete?**

    • **How can *your* joy be complete?**

Have partners share their lists with each other. Ask partners to tell each other what part each listed item plays in their joy level. Then have partners pray for each other in each specific area, asking God to give them complete joy.

Kindness

Rómulo Sauñe (1953–1992)

Read the following true story aloud to your students, or ask a student to read it aloud.

Despite the threat of the Shining Path, Rómulo Sauñe had spent several weeks selling more than eleven thousand Bibles at a discounted price to the people of Ayacucho, Peru. The Shining Path was one of the most brutal terrorist groups in the Western Hemisphere, and it violently opposed Christian missionaries. In fact, Sauñe's own grandfather had been brutally murdered by the terrorist group.

One night after Sauñe had finished distributing the Bibles, he put his children to bed and heard a knock at the door.

"Who is it?" Sauñe asked.

"Is the pastor there?" the voice returned.

The pastor of the church had left for the night, so Sauñe told the visitor, "He's not here." And the visitor walked away into the night.

The next morning Sauñe heard another knock at the door. He opened the door and found a man standing there with a gunny sack over his shoulder.

"Good morning," Sauñe greeted.

"Is the pastor here?" the man returned.

"No, the pastor doesn't live here. Why do you ask?" questioned Sauñe.

"Why didn't you open the door last night?" inquired the man. "If you had, things would have been quite different. I came by with two of my comrades. We were going to kill you…I've worked hard in recent months spying on the church. I even memorized Bible verses so you would think I was a part of the congregation. But I've also taught other comrades how to set dynamite and destroy churches."

"Why are you telling me this?" asked Sauñe.

"Last night I was tortured by those Bible verses that I had learned," replied the man. "They were like a hammer pounding inside my head. Finally I couldn't stand it anymore. So this morning I decided to talk with you about your faith, about your God."

Sauñe sat down next to the man. With gentleness, Sauñe taught the man about Christianity, prayed with the man, and comforted the man as he cried. In celebration, the man gave Sauñe the gunny sack, which contained his gun and his ammunition.

(Adapted from Ambassadors for Christ: Distinguished Representatives of the Message Throughout the World, *edited by John D. Woodbridge.)*

Discussion Starter

Ask:

• **Why do you think Rómulo Sauñe was able to reach the heart of a hardened terrorist?**

• **Would you have treated the terrorist with the same kindness Rómulo Sauñe showed him? Why or why not?**

Read Luke 6:27-31 aloud.

Say: **Kindness is a powerful weapon. One of the most powerful and shocking things you can do is show kindness toward someone who hurts you or attacks you. As we've seen in Rómulo Sauñe's story, kindness combined with God's Word can lead a hardened terrorist to Christ.**

Have teenagers form trios to help each other come up with "conspiracies of kindness." Have each person in the trio target someone to be kind to. Then have the other group members help the student come up with a plan that will effectively communicate kindness to the targeted person. After each person has a plan, have trios pray for the people they're targeting.

Sidelight

In September 1992, while returning home from a village outside Ayacucho, Rómulo Sauñe was stopped by a roadblock set up by the Shining Path. After shooting and killing Sauñe, one of the terrorists shouted, "We got him!"

Leadership

Florence Nightingale (1820–1910)

Read the following true story aloud to your students, or ask a student to read it aloud.

During the Crimean War, which began in 1853, more soldiers died of disease than wounds. Filthy conditions characterized the military hospitals. Soldiers who came to the hospitals often found sickness and death instead of help and health. When news of the hospital conditions made it to England, the government called for volunteer nurses. One of those answering the call was Florence Nightingale.

At the time, nursing was not a respected profession. So when Nightingale arrived at the hospital, the military doctors refused to cooperate with the determined woman. But the conditions became so bad and the barracks were so full and dirty, they had no choice but to give Nightingale charge. The first order she issued was for two hundred scrub brushes. She and the other nurses worked like slaves to clean the military hospital. After cleaning the hospital every day, and after the other medical staff had left for bed, Nightingale would visit the sick and dying soldiers while carrying a small lamp to light her way.

Nightingale's care and hard work at the hospital were noticed by the British government as well as the public. So the government sent her to Crimea to care for more wounded soldiers. While there, Nightingale demanded full authority over *all* the female nurses in the British army—and she got it! Nightingale reformed the entire medical corps, making cleanliness and compassion top priorities. Her efforts changed the effectiveness of the British hospitals and changed medicine throughout the world by demonstrating the necessity of sanitary conditions.

Sidelight

The only reward Florence Nightingale ever accepted for her work was the British Order of Merit. She was blind and senile as the award was placed in her hands. "Too kind, too kind," the eighty-seven-year-old woman responded.

After the war, Nightingale shifted her focus to public medicine. She established the world's first school of nursing. She created programs for training midwives, for preparing special nurses for workhouses, and for improving public sanitation. She even wrote a nursing textbook.

Through the years, Nightingale never looked for a reward for her work. "Christ is the author of our profession," she once told a group of nurses. Nightingale believed the work she did as a nurse provided her with an opportunity to show Christ's mercy to others. She believed God had called her to work and lead others to serve, rather than to look for a reward.

(Adapted from Holy Company: Christian Heroes and Heroines *by Elliott Wright.)*

Discussion Starter

Have teenagers form groups of four. Give each group a sheet of newsprint and a marker. Say: **With your group, decide who you think is the world's greatest leader (other than Jesus). The person doesn't necessarily have to be famous. He or she should just be a great leader. And he or she can be a past or present leader. Write that person's name at the top of your newsprint. Under the leader's name, make a list of all the qualities that make the person a great leader. On the back of your sheet, do the same thing with the world's worst leader. Just make sure none of us personally know the person you choose as the worst.**

Give each group an opportunity to share the characteristics of its worst leader. Then have groups tape their sheets to the walls with the characteristics of the greatest leaders facing out.

Read Luke 22:24-26 aloud. Ask:

• **As you look at the leaders around our room, how do they compare to the type of leadership Jesus spoke of?**

• **How do these leaders compare with Florence Nightingale? with Jesus?**

Sidelight

Florence Nightingale was in poor health for much of her life. She spent the last fifty-three years of her life as an invalid. During this time, she accomplished much of her work in reforming the military and civilian health-care systems.

Sidelight

Florence Nightingale's family was strongly opposed to her desire of becoming a nurse, since the nursing profession was not held in high esteem. But Nightingale followed what she believed to be a calling from God to "devote [herself] to the sick and sorrowful."

• How does the world's understanding of leadership compare with God's explanation?

Say: **Leaders should be decisive. They must have vision and focus. But more than anything else, a true leader is a servant. Jesus was, of course, the greatest leader who ever lived. He showed us what a true leader is like by dying for us. Florence Nightingale was a decisive and strong leader. But she was an effective leader because she was also a servant.**

Love

Mother Teresa (1910–1997)

Read the following true story aloud to your students, or ask a student to read it aloud.

At age eighteen, Agnes Gonxha Bojaxhiu made a vow to the church and God as she joined the Sisters of Our Lady of Loreto. There she re-named herself Teresa. She would later become known as Mother Teresa.

Teresa spent seventeen years teaching at an elite private school in Calcutta, India. She then became sick and went to Darjeeling, India, to recuperate. "It was in the train I heard the call to give up all and fol-low [God] to the slums to serve him among the poorest of the poor," she recalled.

Mother Teresa began teaching children in the slums of Calcutta. It was in front of a hospital in Calcutta that Mother Teresa found a woman "half-eaten by maggots and rats." Mother Teresa sat with the woman until she died. Soon after-ward, Mother Teresa began her own order—the Mis-sionaries of Charity.

Teresa's work was desperately needed in India as most of the people didn't reach out to others in need. The Hindus believed that people should live out their place in society, whether or not they were impover-ished and sick. "They lived like animals," said Mother Teresa. "At least they can die like human beings."

Mother Teresa's influence and work began to grow. She helped the lepers of India. She fed the hun-gry of Ethiopia, cared for radiation victims of the Cher-nobyl nuclear accident, created a global network of homes for the poor, and founded one of the first homes for AIDS victims. Mother Teresa was given nu-merous awards for her loving care, including the No-bel Peace Prize.

Despite her fame and influence, Mother Teresa continued caring

Sidelight

After Mother Teresa joined the Sisters of Our Lady of Loreto, her brother sent her a letter warning, "Do you realize that you are burying yourself?" Teresa an-swered, "You think you are so important, as an official serving the king of two million subjects. Well, I am an official, too, serving the King of the whole world."

for the unloved and wearing a sari that cost one dollar until her death in 1997 at the age of eighty-seven.

(Adapted from ABCNEWS.com [more.abcnews.go.com/sections/world/teresa_bio/index.html].)

Discussion Starter

Have teenagers form trios, and give each trio a sheet of paper and a pen or pencil. Say: **With your group, I'd like you to come up with a definition of the word "love." The definition must not include the word "love," and it must be something the three of you can agree upon.**

Sidelight
While dearly loved by the public, Mother Teresa was criticized by some because of her conservative values. She especially came under fire for arguing against abortion, contraception, and divorce.

Allow groups to share their definitions, and then say: **I'm going to ask you a few questions that I want you to answer silently to yourself. For each question, use the definition of love your trio came up with to answer it.** Read Matthew 5:43-48 aloud. Ask:

• **Have you ever been dumped by a boyfriend or girlfriend? Do you love that person?**

• **Have you ever been stabbed in the back by a friend? Do you love that person?**

• **Have you ever been made fun of or ridiculed? Do you love the person who did it?**

• **Have you ever been overlooked, ignored, or undervalued by someone? Do you love that person?**

• **Have you ever seen a homeless person who was stumbling around drunk? Do you love that person?**

• **Think of the person in this world you like the least. Do you love that person?**

Have teenagers open their Bibles to 1 Corinthians 13. Say: **You may not feel love for some of the people you thought about. And that's OK. Because love isn't a feeling. Love is a choice that leads to action. Of course, it's important to work through feelings of bitterness and anger and attitudes of unforgiveness. But you can do that while choosing to love a person the entire time. Look at 1 Corinthians 13:4-13. None of the verses say that love is a warm feeling. The verses just show what love chooses to do.**

Think about the person in your life who is hardest to love. You can

be patient with the person. You can be kind to the person. You can re-fuse to keep a record of that person's wrongs. You can protect and hope in the person. You can do all these things no matter *how* you *feel*.

Mother Teresa loved the unlovable. She chose to care for the sick and dying. She loved prostitutes and outcasts. She understood that love is a choice that leads to action. I'd like you to take a minute and quietly think about the people in your life you need to love—even if you don't want to.

Give teenagers one minute to think, and then allow volunteers to dis-cuss what they thought about.

Loyalty

Dietrich Bonhoeffer (1906–1945)

Read the following true story aloud to your students, or ask a student to read it aloud.

Many people know of Dietrich Bonhoeffer for his stance against Hitler that led to his execution in a concentration camp. But people are less familiar with Bonhoeffer's time in the United States. The young German came to New York to attend Union Theological Seminary. While there, he became close friends with Franklin Fisher.

In Germany, Bonhoeffer had hardly seen black people. But he and Fisher, an African-American student from Birmingham, Alabama, became close friends. Fisher was assigned to the Abyssinian Baptist Church in Harlem for his field work, and Bonhoeffer accompanied him there by teaching Sunday school.

Sidelight

Dietrich Bonhoeffer was a double agent during World War II. He served in Hitler's military-intelligence organization while smuggling Jews into Switzerland and doing other underground tasks.

The experience helped Bonhoeffer see the realities of life in Harlem as he encountered the city's severe problems with racism. Spending time with Fisher and members of the church helped Bonhoeffer see beyond race and love his African-American friends as brothers and sisters. But his loyalty to his friends was put to the test by the racist attitudes around him.

While Bonhoeffer, Fisher, and a few friends were eating in a restaurant, Bonhoeffer noticed that Fisher wasn't receiving the same service he was. This type of prejudice was quite prevalent at the time. And it would have been quite normal for Bonhoeffer to do nothing about it. Instead, Bonhoeffer stood up for his friends. In a fury, he protested the treatment of his friends and immediately left the restaurant in disgust and anger.

When Bonhoeffer left New York, he took memories of Fisher and Harlem with him. After an evening of playing spirituals for his German friends and students, Bonhoeffer said, "When I took leave of my black friend, he said to me, 'Make our sufferings known in Germany, tell them what is happening to us, and show them what we are like.' I wanted to fulfill this obligation tonight."

Perhaps it was in Harlem where Bonhoeffer learned that being true to God and loved ones was more important than the opinions of others. Maybe his experiences in Harlem gave him the strength to oppose Hitler by helping the Jews in Germany and remaining loyal to them and God to the point of death.

(Adapted from Christian History magazine, Volume 10, Number 4.)

Discussion Starter

Have teenagers form groups of four. Say: **With your group, I'd like you to discuss what you would do if you were in the following situation.**

Kerry has been your friend since grade school. He's a great guy, but he's just a little insecure. He says things that embarrass you and cause others to make fun of him. Like last week at the assembly, where the speaker was doing a demonstration on hang gliding. When the demonstration was over and the speaker asked for questions, Kerry stood up, put his arms out, and shouted, "Theoretically, if I flapped my arms fast enough, wouldn't I be able to fly without a hang glider?" He started laughing hysterically. No one else thought it was funny. And you're starting to wonder if you should distance yourself from Kerry just a bit.

Sidelight

Dietrich Bonhoeffer's parents didn't learn of his execution until more than three months after his death. They first heard of their son's death while listening to a radio broadcast from London of a memorial service for their son.

Ask:

• **How would you react to this situation?**

• **How *should* you react?**

• **Read Proverbs 17:17. How does this passage apply to this situation?**

• **What would Dietrich Bonhoeffer have done in this situation?**

• **What would Jesus do?**

Say: **Loyalty to others is a precious thing today. It's easy to stick by someone when things are going well. But you find out what you're made** of when a friend is going through a tough time. Of course, our first loyalty goes to Jesus. But we must be loyal to one another. We must support others even when they make fools of themselves or appear to be falling apart. In fact, those are the times when others need us the most. Wouldn't you agree?

Mercy

Callistus I (birth date unknown; died 222)

Read the following true story aloud to your students, or ask a student to read it aloud.

Callistus had humble beginnings. He was a slave in second-century Rome—and it appears that Callistus had a difficult time doing that. His master, Carporphorus, had entrusted money to him, and through bad investments, Callistus lost it all. After Callistus lost his master's money, he ran away to avoid punishment. Carporphorus caught up with him and had him imprisoned.

Carporphorus eventually took pity on Callistus and had him set free on the condition that Callistus would try to get the money back. Callistus failed in his efforts and resorted to bursting into a synagogue and shouting for money. Callistus was quickly arrested again for his actions.

For political reasons, Emperor Commodus freed many Christians who had been arrested—and Callistus was one of them. The church took Callistus in, and eventually Pope Zephyrinus put him in charge of a Christian cemetery. Callistus proved faithful and trustworthy to Zephyrinus, so the pope made Callistus a deacon. After Zephyrinus died, the Christian church in Rome voted Callistus as the new pope! God's amazing mercy was evident in Callistus' life; the slave and criminal had become the pope!

There's no doubt that God's mercy toward Callistus caused him to be a merciful pope. A leader in the church named Hippolytus believed that people who committed adultery or murder should be forever excluded from taking Communion. As pope, Callistus decreed that the people who had committed such acts and did public penance were welcome to participate. Hippolytus was furious at Callistus. He attacked and undermined the pope in everything he did. In fact, Hippolytus set *himself* up as pope in reaction to Callistus' merciful stance.

Sidelight

When it comes to the story of Callistus and Hippolytus, it's difficult to know exactly what the whole truth was. The only surviving record of Callistus was written by a man who hated him—Hippolytus himself.

Despite the attacks from Hippolytus, Callistus continued his support of and belief in mercy. He allowed the worst of sinners to return to the church. As further evidence of Callistus' mercy, he never attacked or rebuked Hippolytus—even though as pope, he was the most powerful man in the church.

(Adapted from Holy Company: Christian Heroes and Heroines *by Elliott Wright, and the Catholic Online Web site [www.catholic.org/saints/calistus.html].)*

Discussion Starter

Give each student a sheet of paper and a pen or pencil. Say: **Callistus probably was able to show mercy to others because God had shown him so much mercy. I'd like you to get in touch with God's mercy by looking at what your life would have been like so far if God had not been involved in any way. Write a short autobiography that tells your life story as if God had little or no hand in it.**

Give teenagers about ten minutes to write, and then allow volunteers to share their stories. Read Luke 6:36 aloud. Ask:

• **What are some examples of God's mercy in your life?**

• **According the passage I just read, what does this say about how you should treat others?**

• **What does it mean to show mercy?**

• **Are you a merciful person?**

• **How can you become more merciful?**

Say: **God has shown us the ultimate mercy. God loved us and saved us while we were sinners and in rebellion against God. Jesus tells us to be merciful just as *God* is merciful. God has forgiven us for so much, we must forgive others when they make mistakes or sin against us. I challenge you to follow Jesus' words and Callistus' example by showing the kind of mercy God has shown you.**

Obedience

Eric Liddell (1902–1945)

Read the following true story aloud to your students, or ask a student to read it aloud.

When Eric Liddell ran, he tilted his head back and looked at the sky. When someone jokingly asked him how he knew where the finish line was, he replied, "The Lord guides me."

Liddell qualified to run for Great Britain in the 1924 Olympics by winning the 220-yard dash and the 100-yard dash at the London AAA Championships. In fact, his time in the 100-yard dash stood as a record for the next thirty-five years.

Liddell would be running in the Olympics in Paris. He planned to compete in a number of races, but his best event was the 100-meter. In that race, Liddell was considered a strong contender for Olympic gold.

Liddell and the other runners waited excitedly to see when they would run. When the schedule of events was posted, Liddell couldn't believe his eyes. The preliminary races for the 100-meter sprint, 4x100 relay, and 4x400 relay—his best events—were on Sunday.

Eric Liddell took very seriously God's command to keep the Sabbath. He believed Sunday was a sacred day that should be set aside for the Lord. "I'm not running," Liddell explained.

Sidelight

In 1932, Eric Liddell was ordained a minister. He spent the remainder of his life as a missionary in China.

Even though he risked disapproval and pressure from others, Eric Liddell didn't change his mind. As the Olympic runners raced to qualify in the 100-meter sprint, Liddell was preaching in a Paris church. He felt that God didn't want him to run on Sunday, and he obeyed. Later, Liddell had a chance to race in the 200-meter and 400-meter sprints. But they weren't his best races, and he wasn't expected to do well in either. Amazingly, Liddell won a bronze medal in the 200-meter sprint and won a *gold* medal in the 400-meter! In fact, he set a world record of 47.6 seconds!

(Adapted from an In Touch Ministries Web site about Eric Liddell [www.intouch.org/INTOUCH/portraits/eric_liddell.html].)

Discussion Starter

If you have time, watch the movie *Chariots of Fire* with your group. The movie is based on Eric Liddell's life and faith. If you don't have enough time to watch the movie, either start the devotion with the following questions or watch pertinent clips of the movie, starting with Liddell's decision not to run. After the movie, discuss Liddell's obedience and conviction and how others reacted to his decisions. Then ask:

- **Do you think Eric Liddell made the right choice? Why or why not?**
- **Would you have made the same choice Liddell made? Explain.**

Say: **Eric Liddell believed Sunday was a day of rest, and he obeyed God's command to keep the Sabbath. Some may say Liddell's interpretation of the Sabbath was too strict. Whether it was or it wasn't, I'm impressed with Liddell's willingness to be obedient.**

Sidelight

When Eric Liddell died of a brain tumor at the age of forty-three, his last words were, "It's complete surrender." Those words accurately describe his attitude toward and devotion to God.

I'm going to ask you a series of questions that I'd like you to answer silently. I'll give you about thirty seconds after each question. Seriously consider each question, and spend any remaining time you have talking to God about your heart. I'll begin the questions by reading Jesus' words in Matthew 10:37-39.

Read Matthew 10:37-39 aloud, and then ask each of the following questions. Make sure you give teenagers thirty seconds of reflection time after each question.

- **Would you obey Christ if it meant giving up your favorite hobby or extracurricular activity?**
- **Would you obey Christ if it meant losing all your friends?**
- **Would you obey Christ if it meant giving up your dreams?**
- **Would you obey Christ if it meant losing your family?**
- **Would you obey Christ if it meant dying for him?**
- **Do you obey Christ now?**

End the devotion by saying: **In Jesus' name, amen.**

Passion

Keith Green (1954–1982)

Read the following true story aloud to your students, or ask a student to read it aloud.

Everything Keith Green did was all or nothing. Just after he became a Christian, Keith took every opportunity he could to tell others about Jesus. He and his wife, Melody, made an effort to reach out to runaways and unmarried pregnant women. The couple took in people who were homeless and on drugs. Keith and Melody spent almost every night at Bible studies, and Keith often stayed up all night counseling people who came to him with problems. Melody later described Keith as "the most energetic person I'd ever met in my whole life."

Keith channeled his passion for Christ into passionate music. In albums such as *No Compromise,* Keith challenged Christians to live passionate lives for Christ with lyrics such as: "How can you be so dead, when you've been so well-fed?"

Just as Keith was becoming a Christian music celebrity, he felt God directing him to perform a three-day concert on the campus of Oral Roberts University. The first two evenings of the concert went just as planned. Many people showed up, and many responded to the message Keith presented. But Keith knew God wasn't finished. He believed the campus of ORU was in need of Christians who lived passionate and pure lives for Christ. And Keith believed the answer was found in repentance.

Sidelight

At the age of 28, Keith Green died in a plane crash along with two of his children.

On the third night of the concert, Keith opened to the packed arena with worship, prayer, and praises. Then Keith boldly presented what he felt was the purpose of the three-day event. He shared a list of sins that were prevalent on the ORU campus. He called for people in the audience to confess their sins, to turn from their ways, and to live for Christ. Crowds of people came forward as Keith continued playing the piano, looking up, and crying out for God to break the hearts of the people.

He opened the microphone to allow people to confess their sins.

Young men and women began stepping up to the microphone with surface confessions of breaking curfew and living false Christianity. As the night went on, the confessions became much more personal and significant. People repented of drug use, sexual immorality, and homosexuality. Meanwhile, Keith crawled under his piano and prayed. Keith wanted the people to focus on God and getting right with God rather than listening to his music or focusing on him. Keith's bold and passionate challenge changed the face of the ORU campus.

(Adapted from It's My Turn: How You Can Be Mentored by Christianity's Greatest Leaders, *compiled by Kingdom Building Ministries, and the Last Days Ministries Web site [www.lastdaysministries.org].)*

Discussion Starter

Ask students:

• **What do you think of Keith Green?**

• **Is passion a good thing or a bad thing? Explain.**

• **Have you ever met someone who was passionate about his or her relationship with Christ? If so, what was that person like?**

• **Are you passionate about your relationship with Christ?**

• **How can we become passionate about serving and knowing God?**

Have teenagers form a circle, and place a bowl full of sand in the middle of the circle. Read Deuteronomy 6:4-5 aloud. Then cup both your

hands together, and ask a volunteer to fill your hands with sand.

Say: **We're going to pass this sand around the circle. When you pass the sand to the person next to you, say: "Love the Lord your God with all your heart, all your soul, and all your strength."**

Pass the sand to the person next to you, and say: [Person's name]**, love the Lord your God with *all* your heart, *all* your soul, and *all* your strength.** Wait for the sand to be passed around the circle. Then ask:

• **What happened to the sand as it was passed around the circle?**

• **How does this exercise demonstrate what it means to be a Christian who is passionate about Christ?**

• **How does a person's passion for Christ affect other people?**

• **How can you tell if someone is loving God with all of his or her heart, soul, and strength?**

Say: **You can tell when you've encountered a Christian who is passionate about his or her relationship with Christ because the person rubs off on you just like the sand did. You can tell when you're passionate about your relationship with Christ because your passion rubs off on others. Keith Green was passionate about his relationship with Christ. His passion came through in his music and even in the way he conducted his concerts. Let your passion for Jesus shine through in everything you do so Christ can rub off on others through you.**

Patience

John Calvin (1509–1564)

Read the following true story aloud to your students, or ask a student to read it aloud.

John Calvin was a busy man. He was a pastor who was reforming the church in Geneva, Switzerland, and challenging the Church around the world. And challenging the Church occupies just about all of a person's time. Calvin constantly argued and debated his positions. He had to deal with vicious attacks from those who disagreed with and were threatened by his beliefs. Calvin just didn't have time for relationships or a wife.

So John Calvin didn't involve himself in romantic interests. He was content to preach, debate, and pastor—until he met Martin and Elizabeth Bucer. The Bucers had a wonderful marriage. Calvin couldn't help but notice that the two of them made each other incredibly happy. And Martin Bucer was so excited about his own marriage that he took it upon himself to help everyone else get married—including John Calvin.

Sidelight

Idelette died when John Calvin was forty.

It was after spending time with the Bucers that Calvin decided to find a wife. He believed he needed someone to help him in ministry, to care for him, and to keep him from feeling alone. So Calvin told his friends he was beginning his search. True to Calvin's practical and rational mind, he conducted his search like a manager looking for employees. He even set a date for the ceremony before he was engaged!

Sidelight

Idelette came into the marriage with John Calvin with two children. After their marriage, John and Idelette lost two children to premature birth and one who died at birth.

His first candidate was a wealthy woman from Germany. During the "interview" process, Calvin was disappointed to learn that she didn't know French and that she was a little too wealthy for his liking. The second candidate spoke French, but she was fifteen years older than he was—Calvin quickly lost interest. The third candidate also spoke French, and she was poor—it seemed to be a perfect match. Calvin wrote to a friend named William Farel, explaining that the ceremony would take place before mid-March. But as the two got to know each other, the relationship fell apart.

Calvin became dejected and disappointed. He wrote Farel again, saying, "I have not found a wife and frequently hesitate as to whether I ought any more to seek one." And Calvin stopped looking. It was when Calvin stopped trying to make a marriage happen that God brought him a wife. He fell for a young widow in his congregation named Idelette de Bure Stordeur. She was intelligent, was cultured, and had a strong love for the Lord. Calvin wrote again to his friend William Farel. This time, Farel responded to Calvin's letter by officiating John and Idelette's wedding ceremony.

(Adapted from Christian History magazine, Volume 5, Number 4.)

Discussion Starter

Say: **We're going to conduct an experiment. I'd like you to sit absolutely still and absolutely quiet. Don't look at your watch. Don't talk to anyone. Just look straight ahead. Continue doing this until I let you know the experiment is over. Ready? Begin.**

Wait for at least two minutes, then ask:

• **How long do you think you were required to wait?**

• **How did it feel to sit there and wait?**

• **Why is waiting so difficult for us?**

• **Why do you think John Calvin had to wait longer than he wanted to before he found a wife?**

> **Sidelight**
> John Calvin hated to waste time. On his deathbed, Calvin's friends asked him to rest from working. He replied, "What! Would you have the Lord find me idle when he comes?"

Have teenagers form groups of four to discuss these questions:

• **What events or things are you waiting for right now?**

• **Read Romans 11:33-36. How does this passage apply to your situation?**

• **How does John Calvin's story affect the way you look at your situation?**

Say: **You may not be able to understand God's timing concerning the** things you're waiting for—but God's timing is perfect nonetheless. No matter what you need or want, you can know that God will bring you what you need when you need it. All you need to do is wait patiently for God.

Peace

Abraham Lincoln (1809–1865)

Read the following true story aloud to your students, or ask a student to read it aloud.

He stood looking at himself in the mirror, saying, "It's true, Abe Lincoln, you are the ugliest man in the world. If I ever see a man uglier than you, I'm going to shoot him on the spot!"

Abraham Lincoln's life was filled with discontent and sorrow. When he was only nine years old, his mother died. When Lincoln was sixteen, a close boyhood friend went insane. When he was nineteen, his sister, Sarah, died. When Lincoln was twenty-six years old, his fiancée died. After his fiancée's death, Lincoln said, "There is nothing to live for now." And when Lincoln was forty-one, his second son, Eddie, died after a long illness.

As a politician, Lincoln was under constant political attack and pressure. Before his inauguration, Lincoln lost forty pounds, he couldn't sleep, he was often threatened by his political enemies, and he was certain he wouldn't return from the presidency alive.

Lincoln's mother taught him to keep God's commandments. But Lincoln could see only where he failed. Lincoln's bodyguard later explained, "The misery that dripped from Lincoln as he walked was caused by his lack of personal faith." Abraham Lincoln knew the Scriptures and believed in Deity. But he failed to realize that righteousness comes from faith alone. Without an understanding of God and a realization of God's forgiveness and presence, Lincoln bore his tragedy alone. Without a close relationship with God, there was no solace or peace for Abraham Lincoln.

It was the death of his dear son Willie that spurred the change. Willie was Lincoln's youngest and favorite

Sidelight

Before he became president, Abraham Lincoln attended a camp meeting led by the Rev. Dr. Peter Akers. "I am not a prophet," Akers declared. "But I am a student of the prophets...American slavery will come to an end in some near decade. I think in the [eighteen] sixties..." Akers then went on to describe a war that would happen in the United States. Akers finished by saying, "Who can tell but that the man who shall lead us through the strife may be standing in this presence." Lincoln described the event by saying, "Those words were from beyond the speaker...The doctor has persuaded me that slavery will go down with the crash of a civil war."

child. While the president grieved, Willie's nurse told Lincoln of her personal relationship with Jesus Christ and encouraged him to know Jesus as Savior.

Lincoln later explained, "When I left Springfield, I asked the people to pray for me; I was not a Christian. When I buried my son—the severest trial of my life—I was not a Christian. But when I went to Gettysburg, and saw the graves of thousands of our soldiers, I then and there consecrated myself to Christ." Lincoln told his friends that giving his life to Christ finally brought the peace he was looking for all his life.

(Adapted from More Than Conquerors: Portraits of Believers From All Walks of Life, *edited by John Woodbridge.)*

Discussion Starter

Give each teenager a sheet of paper and a pen or pencil. Then have students close their eyes. Say: **I'm going to play part of a song for you. I want you to think of the emotions behind the song. I'm really not interested in whether you like the music or if it's well done. I just want you to think about what types of emotions and feelings the music brings to mind.**

Play part of the most peaceful song you can find. For example, you could play a section from an instrumental harp or instrumental saxophone CD. Then have students open their eyes and write the emotions that came to mind.

Say: **I'm going to play another song. Again, don't judge the music on personal taste, just listen for the emotions and feelings the song inspires. Please close your eyes and listen.** Play the most grating and dissonant song you can find as loud as you can. (If you have difficulty finding such a song, ask one of your teenagers for help before the meeting.) After you play a portion of the song, ask teenagers to write the emotions and feelings that came to mind.

Ask:

• **What emotions and feelings did each song inspire?**

Sidelight

Despite the melancholy Abraham Lincoln struggled with, he was a very persistent man. Consider these significant setbacks Lincoln faced before becoming president in 1860:

• 1832—Defeated for Illinois Legislature

• 1843—Defeated for U.S. Congress

• 1848—Defeated for re-election to U.S. Congress (Lincoln won election in 1846)

• 1855—Defeated for U.S. Senate

• 1856—Defeated for U.S. vice-presidential nomination

• 1858—Defeated for U.S. Senate.

- **What is peace?**
- **What kinds of things bring peace? obstruct peace?**
- **What did it take for Abraham Lincoln to find peace?**
- **Do you have the same peace Lincoln found? Explain.**

Read Philippians 4:5-7 aloud. Ask:

- **How can we find the peace these verses describe?**

Have teenagers take turns praying aloud for God's peace. When it appears that everyone who wants to pray has had a chance, pray aloud: **May the peace of God, which transcends all understanding, guard your hearts and minds in Christ Jesus. Amen.**

Perseverance

George Washington (1732–1799)

Read the following true story aloud to your students, or ask a student to read it aloud.

Thirteen thousand men waited for their general near Boston. They had come from the colonies to fight for independence. They were brave men, and they believed in the cause of freedom. But they were also quite inexperienced and undisciplined. They were farmers, townspeople, and family men. Very few had any experience as soldiers. The men came from the various colonies to fight the British for their freedom, and Gen. George Washington came to lead them.

Washington's first challenge was to turn the men into soldiers. Of course he taught them how to march, to shoot, to obey orders, and to fight. But Washington also put them through some unusual "character training." Washington issued orders such as: "All men will attend church services, carrying their arms and ammunition with them." He also ordered that all officers must refrain from swearing. Washington would ride among his men, challenging them to fear God and to practice Christian virtues.

Sidelight

"Mankind, when left to themselves, are unfit for their own government."
—George Washington, 1786.

Washington knew the battles that lay ahead would push the men to the limits of humanity. He knew the men wouldn't survive or win the battles if they had no character. And their character was tested again and again.

One of the most famous tests came at Valley Forge. The Americans had just lost Philadelphia, the capital of the revolutionary government, to the British. Morale was incredibly low, and the full force of winter was soon to come. Rations were scarce. Two thousand of the eleven thousand men were barefoot. The biting cold left footprints of blood for many of these men. Many others had no coats, and no one could stay warm. It was the darkest time of the war for the American troops, and many thought of giving up.

But the character that had been instilled in the men shone through. They spent the winter training and preparing. By the time winter was over, the American army was a fine-tuned machine. Soon the French joined the war as allies to the Americans. Supplies began pouring in, and the tide of the war changed. The ragged men were refreshed and resolved as they marched on to fight for American independence.

(Adapted from The Light and the Glory for Children: Discovering God's Plan for America From Christopher Columbus to George Washington by Peter Marshall and David Manuel.)

Discussion Starter

Have teenagers form two groups. Give each group a stack of paper. Set a small board or a large book in front of one group and a large, upside-down cooking bowl in front of the other. Say: **I'd like each group to create a structure using the paper I've given you as blocks. For example, you can create "blocks" by rolling up sheets of paper or by folding them in half like tents. One group must use the board** (or book) **as the foundation for its structure. The other group must use the upside-down bowl as its foundation. Your goal is to make the structure as sturdy as possible. It also should rise at least twenty-four inches above your foundation.**

After groups build their structures, ask:

Sidelight
George Washington was inconsistent in his church attendance and never participated in the Lord's Supper. However, he wrote in his prayer diary that God would accept him because of what Jesus Christ had done.

• How did the foundation affect your structure's sturdiness?

Read Matthew 7:24-27 aloud. Then ask:

• How do the two structures we built demonstrate this passage?

• What are some sandy foundations people build on today?

• Why do you think George Washington focused on small things such as swearing and church services?

• Do you think these things really had an effect on the Continental Army's ability to persevere through the winter?

Say: **Your ability to persevere is exclusively dependent on your foundation. If your character is built on Christ and strengthened by virtue and righteousness, there's nothing that can knock you over. The Continental Army was able to persevere through the winter because the soldiers had character and a strong foundation. Without that same foundation, you can't stand firm.**

Persistence

Francis Xavier (1506–1552)

Read the following true story aloud to your students, or ask a student to read it aloud.

Francis Xavier was born an aristocrat in the Xavier Castle. His mother was an heiress, and his father was a lawyer and high-ranking government official. Xavier's parents groomed him for a career in the church by sending him to school at the University of Paris and the College of Saint-Barbe.

But Xavier had different plans for his life. He was charming, witty, athletic, musical, handsome, popular with women, and vain. Xavier lost interest in the church and dedicated his youth to finding pleasure.

While Xavier continued in fulfilling his own lusts, his college roommate, Ignatius Loyola, decided that Francis Xavier would make an excellent missionary. Loyola began to share his faith with his roommate. Xavier, of course, ignored his roommate's preaching and didn't want anything to do with Loyola. He thought Loyola was a fanatic and a bigot. Xavier was more interested in sex and gambling than in Christ.

But Loyola refused to give up. He repeatedly asked Xavier to give up his sinful lifestyle and to follow Christ. Loyola also repeatedly quoted Scripture passages to Xavier. But Xavier refused to listen.

Xavier's attitude toward Loyola finally changed when he ran short of funds and Loyola willingly shared his own money with Xavier. The act caused Xavier to start listening to Loyola. Xavier began to notice the monotony and disappointments of his lifestyle and began to seriously consider what Loyola had been saying. During a conversation late at night, Loyola quoted part of Matthew 16:26 to Xavier—"What good will it be for a man if he gains the whole world, yet forfeits his soul?" Xavier finally understood and finally let go. Xavier repented of his sins,

Sidelight

Many miracles are associated with the life of Francis Xavier. One reported miracle tells of Xavier dangling his crucifix into the sea to calm the waters during a voyage. The waves swallowed the crucifix and it was lost in the sea. When the ship completed its voyage twenty-four hours later, Xavier reportedly was met on a beach by a crab that held the crucifix in one of its pincers.

and from that day on, Francis Xavier was a devoted follower of Christ. He later became one of the most important missionaries in the history of the Christian Church.

(Adapted from Great Leaders of the Christian Church, *edited by John D. Woodbridge.)*

Discussion Starter

Have teenagers form groups of four. Give each group a deck of cards. Say: **With your group, create a house of cards. Your goal is to make the house at least four levels tall.**

Give groups about five minutes to make their houses, then ask:

• **What was it like to build your house of cards?**

• **What would it take to build a house of cards ten feet tall?**

• **Do you think you'll ever build a house of cards ten feet tall? Why or why not?**

Say: **It's amazing what some people will persistently work at. People spend hours building gum-wrapper chains, falling-domino lines, card houses, and many other things. All these efforts take persistence and time. As Christians, we have a very high calling that deserves persistent effort and time.**

Ask a volunteer to read Galatians 6:9-10 aloud. Ask:

• **According to this verse, what must Christians persistently work at?**

• **What harvest do you think our persistence will produce?**

• **Why do you think Ignatius Loyola had such persistence with Francis Xavier?**

• Would you have had the same determination Loyola had?

Say: **If Loyola would have given up, Francis Xavier may not have become the great missionary who reached people in India, Japan, and China. When it comes to sharing our faith, it's difficult to get started, much less to be persistent. But it's important to remember that we never know what's going on in someone's heart. Someone might show anger or disinterest on the outside, but the Holy Spirit may be doing incredible work on the inside. All we have to do is keep praying and trying and letting God change us.**

Sidelight

As a missionary, Francis Xavier truly became "all things to all people." While in Goa, Xavier found that he could reach the most people by living in a modest little room in a local hospital. While in India, Xavier wore a torn cassock and a shabby cowl. While in Japan, Xavier wore fancy clothes and walked tall because the Japanese despised poverty and humility.

Reconciliation

John Perkins (born 1930)

Read the following true story aloud to your students, or ask a student to read it aloud.

John Perkins had plenty of reasons to hate white people. Acts of overt racism were common in John's hometown in Mississippi. He and his family endured inferior living conditions, limited opportunity, condescending attitudes, and the constant threat of physical assault. When John was sixteen years old, his own brother was shot and killed by a white deputy while standing outside a movie theater.

After his brother's death, the Perkins family sent John to California for his own safety. John lived quite happily there for some time and started his own family. Despite the relatively tolerant and accepting attitudes Perkins encountered in California, he chose to move his family back to Mississippi. Perkins knew he would face persecution and pain when he returned, but the opportunity to help bring reconciliation to the town of Mendenhall, Mississippi, was worth the risk.

Perkins began the endeavor by standing up against injustices in Mendenhall. White and black volunteers from Perkins' Voice of Calvary ministry peacefully protested together against racial injustice.

In 1970, a young man named Doug, a white volunteer at Voice of Calvary, and a few other students participated in a peaceful protest march against the false arrests of African Americans in Mendenhall. After the protests, Doug and the other students were pulled over by the highway patrol and arrested on false charges.

When news of Doug's arrest reached Perkins, he and a few friends drove to the next county to post bond for Doug and the students. When Perkins and his friends arrived, they were thrown in jail. Several deputy sheriffs and highway patrol officers beat John Perkins and his friends in jail. Perkins was punched and kicked until his eyes were almost swollen shut.

Sidelight

While visiting the church his young son attended, John Perkins became a Christian. After that, Perkins felt God calling him to return to the South, and he did so in the turbulent sixties.

Even though Perkins had endured so much at the hands of white people, he refused to hate them. He dedicated his life to developing Christian community and racial reconciliation. His ministry took in poor people—whether they were black or white. When Perkins' church expanded to another city, it appointed a black pastor *and* a white pastor to lead the congregation together. He founded the Christian Community Development Association, an organization that works to "take the vision of Christian community development and racial reconciliation back to the streets." Perkins knew hate and bitterness would help no one, so he dedicated his life to building understanding and forgiveness between the races. He worked to get people of different races to work together toward the common goal of serving Christ.

(Adapted from Hero Tales, Volume 2: A Family Treasury of True Stories From the Lives of Christian Heroes *by Dave and Neta Jackson, and the Christian Community Development Association Web site [www.netdoor.com/com/rronline/ccda/].)*

Discussion Starter

Ask:

• **What causes prejudice? hate?**

• **How do you think you would have reacted if you were in John Perkins' situation?**

• **How can we foster reconciliation in our schools? church? community?**

Have teenagers form pairs. Say: **I'm going to ask you to have a very private conversation with your partner. This is a time to find help and healing, so it's important that you keep your conversation confidential. The only exception to this is if your partner tells you something that makes you feel that there is possible danger to your partner or others. In that case, you should talk to me or another person in authority.**

Tell your partner about an area in your heart that needs reconciliation. It can be an area of racial reconciliation, such as subtle attitudes toward different types of people, or personal reconciliation, such as anger toward a person who hurt you. Once your partner has shared with you, ask questions that help your partner explain why he or she feels that way and how God feels about the attitudes.

Read 1 Peter 1:22-23 aloud, and then have partners begin sharing.

Then say: **With your partner, I want you to come up with a step for reconciliation. Help each other think of one action you could take to be reconciled to the people or person you have negative attitudes toward. Then pray together for God's help, healing, and complete reconciliation.**

Resolution

Fanny Crosby (1820–1915)

Read the following true story aloud to your students, or ask a student to read it aloud.

When she was six weeks old, Fanny Crosby caught a slight cold in her eyes. The family doctor was away, so the Crosbys called in a country doctor who they later found out had no qualifications. The doctor ordered hot mustard poultices to be put on Fanny's eyes. The treatment ruined her eyesight. When Fanny was five years old, her mother took her to a prominent eye specialist. After examining her, the doctor gave the diagnosis: "Poor child, I am afraid you will never see again."

Many people looked at her with pity, but Fanny didn't think she was a "poor child." When she was just eight years old, she wrote this poem:

Sidelight
Fanny Crosby would create up to seven poems or hymns a day! More than once, when Fanny heard a hymn she liked and asked who wrote it, she found out she was the author.

> O what a happy soul am I! Although I cannot see,
> I am resolved that in this world, contented I will be.
> How many blessings I enjoy, that other people don't.
> To weep and sigh because I'm blind, I cannot and I won't!

Fanny resolved to never let her loss of sight serve as an excuse. And she always made the best of the situation. For example, instead of lamenting that she couldn't read, she studied the Bible and poetry by committing large amounts to memory. It's quite probable that Fanny had the first five books of the Bible, the book of Ruth, Psalms, Proverbs, Song of Solomon, and much of the New Testament committed to memory. Fanny attended the New York School for the Blind, where she studied grammar, philosophy, astronomy, and political economy.

Her studies and her resolve enabled her to become a famous poet and a hymn writer. She had the

Sidelight
Fanny Crosby hated math, as demonstrated in the following rhyme she created: "I loathe, abhor, it makes me sick / To hear the word Arithmetic."

discipline to write almost nine thousand hymns, including "Blessed Assurance" and "All the Way My Savior Leads Me." In fact, Fanny Crosby's determination and writing skill made her one of the most famous women in nineteenth-century America. She even became friends with President Grover Cleveland and President Martin Van Buren.

Fanny's resolution certainly had paid off. She once explained, "If perfect earthly sight were offered to me tomorrow, I would not accept it...Although it may have been a blunder on the physician's part, it was no mistake of God's. I...believe it was his intention that I should live my days in physical darkness, so as to be better prepared to sing his praises and incite others so to do. I could not have written thousands of hymns...if I had been hindered by the distractions of seeing all the interesting and beautiful objects that would have been presented to my notice."

(Adapted from More Than Conquerors: Portraits of Believers From All Walks of Life, *edited by John Woodbridge, and* The Christian Connection *Web site [www.webzonecom.com/ccn/].)*

Discussion Starter

Ask:

- **What do you think of Fanny Crosby?**
- **How do you think she could be so determined and so positive in the midst of difficult circumstances?**

Say: **We all face setbacks. Some of us aren't loved by our families as we should be. Some of us are uncoordinated. Some of us have to work harder at school. But we all have one thing in common—we can resolve to overcome our weaknesses and setbacks. Take a minute to think silently about your greatest setback. How does it affect your life?**

Sidelight

Fanny Crosby refused to accept large payments for her speaking or writing. She chose to live simply even though she easily could have become a very wealthy woman.

Read Deuteronomy 30:19-20. Ask:

- **How does this verse apply to setbacks?**

Give each student an index card and a pen or pencil. Say: **No matter what you're facing or what you've gone through, you can resolve in your heart to follow God and to choose life in all you do. For some of you, the choice may be more difficult, but we all can make that choice. Today is a new day. You no longer have to live under your setback or weakness. If you resolve to work through your setbacks and** weaknesses and look to God for strength and support, you can over-come them. You can live for God and serve God in strength and victory.

I want you to make a new-day resolution. Think about how you're going to overcome your setback. Start with the small steps you're going to take this week while keeping your long-term goal in mind. You can simply talk that over with God or write it on your index card.

Give teenagers plenty of time to make their resolutions, and make sure the group prays for any needs that arise.

Resourcefulness
Mary McLeod Bethune (1875–1955)

Read the following true story aloud to your students, or ask a student to read it aloud.

In 1904, Daytona, Florida, was filled with workers who had migrated to find work on the railroads. The town was filthy, the people were poor, and education was a low priority. But Mary McLeod Bethune was ready for the challenge. She wanted to reach and teach children in Daytona, so she went there to open a school. Her school had few students and even less money; Bethune coped by making benches out of boxes and ink out of elderberries. For the first session, Bethune's son and five girls were the only students.

As the school grew, Bethune bought an abandoned garbage dump known as "Hell Hole." During the next two years, it became the permanent site of Bethune's school for black girls, and enrollment reached 250 students. To help pay for tuition at the private school, students would fish in the morning, prepare their catch, and make fish sandwiches to sell to railroad workers. Bethune financed a large portion of the school herself by baking and selling thousands of sweet potato pies.

Sidelight

Mary McLeod Bethune wanted to become a missionary in Africa, but she couldn't find a mission board to support her. One letter of rejection stated, "There are no openings in Africa for black missionaries."

One of the greatest challenges the school faced came from the Ku Klux Klan. Bethune had encouraged other black and female community members to vote in the upcoming elections. And the school concentrated on educating black girls. Needless to say, the Klan wasn't happy with Bethune's activities.

On the night before a 1920 mayoral election, the Klan attempted to intimidate Bethune and everyone she influenced to vote. The Klan cut the electrical power in the neighborhood of the school. At least one hundred men robed in white came marching and riding to the center of the campus. But Bethune kept her cool. The school had its own electrical system, and Bethune ordered the lights to be shut off.

When the men gathered at the school, Bethune had the spotlights on top of the school turned on to illuminate the Klansmen. One young woman began singing a worship song. The women of the entire campus joined in. Surprised and confused, the Klan retreated. Bethune later became known as the "teacher who tamed the Klan."

The next day Bethune made sure there was a high turnout of black voters in the mayoral election. She encouraged people to go to the polls. Once they were there, Bethune distributed cold lemonade as they waited in line. When the day was over, the Klan-endorsed candidate lost the election!

(Adapted from Ambassadors for Christ: Distinguished Representatives of the Message Throughout the World, *edited by John D. Woodbridge.)*

Discussion Starter

Have teenagers form groups of four. Give each group a stack of paper. Say: **With your group, create a game. It can be an active game, a thinking game, or any type of game you like. The only criterion is that your game must use at least one sheet of paper as the central element for the game.**

If students have difficulty coming up with game ideas, suggest the following: folding a sheet of paper into a paper "football," bending or rolling the paper and racing to make paper towers, or tearing a sheet of paper into puzzle pieces. After about five minutes, let each team demonstrate the game it came up with.

Say: **You created some very interesting games. You demonstrated that with resourcefulness, we can do some pretty amazing things with very few resources. Mary McLeod Bethune understood resourcefulness. She used what she had—even though it was very little—to create a school and also to turn back the Klan. As Christians, we can use whatever God puts in front of us to glorify God.**

Read 1 Peter 4:10-11 aloud. Then say: **It's so easy to get caught up in what we don't have. But God has given each of us great gifts. We need to follow Mary McLeod Bethune's example and creatively use those gifts for God's glory.**

Selflessness

Maximilian Kolbe (1894–1941)

Read the following true story aloud to your students, or ask a student to read it aloud.

In four years, more than four million people died at the Auschwitz concentration camp in Poland. Father Maximilian Kolbe was just one of the four million, but the way he died is truly incredible and inspirational.

After Germany invaded Poland in World War II, Kolbe set to the task of taking care of the physical, spiritual, and educational needs of three thousand Polish people—half of whom were Jews. The Nazis declared that education outside Nazi supervision was illegal. Father Kolbe was arrested for running a school and was taken to the Auschwitz concentration camp.

While Kolbe was at Auschwitz, a fellow prisoner escaped from the camp. To discourage future escape attempts, the Nazi guards took revenge on the escapee's family, friends, and fellow prisoners. The prisoners of Auschwitz were lined up outside the barracks as Nazi guards singled out people who would die to pay for the escape.

A Polish sergeant named Franciszek Gajowniczek was one of the men selected for execution. "My poor wife and children!" Gajowniczek screamed as he pleaded with the guards for mercy. Suddenly a slight figure stepped out of line, took off his cap, and stood before the Nazi guards.

"What does this Polish pig want? Who are you?" barked a guard.

"I am a Catholic priest. I want to die for that man; I am old; he has a wife and children," replied Kolbe.

The guard agreed to the priest's request. Maximilian Kolbe, at the age of 47, was executed on August 14, 1941, in place of the Polish sergeant.

Sidelight

In October 1982, Father Maximilian Kolbe was canonized as a saint by Pope John Paul II. Franciszek Gajowniczek attended the ceremony.

(Adapted from Saint of Auschwitz: The Story of Maximilian Kolbe *by Diana Dewar.)*

Discussion Starter

Have teenagers form groups of four. Give each student a sheet of paper and a pen or pencil. Say: **On your sheet of paper, I'd like you to list everything in your life that's important to you.**

After about a minute, instruct teenagers to turn their papers over and list, in order, the five most important things in their lives. Say: **Share the five things you listed with the members of your group. As you share each item, tell the people in your group whether you'd being willing to die for the person or thing you listed. Explain why you would or wouldn't be willing to die for the person or thing.**

After groups share their lists, have them discuss the following questions:

• **What kinds of things are worth dying for?**

• **Why do you think Father Maximilian Kolbe was willing to die for the person the Nazi guards had singled out?**

• **Would you have offered your life to save the prisoner? Why or why not?**

• **Read John 15:13-17. How can we follow Jesus' example of laying down our lives for others?**

Say: **You may never have to decide if you would give your life for someone else. But you have a daily opportunity to decide if you will lay down your life for others. You can decide if you will follow the example of Jesus and the example of Father Kolbe every day. You follow their example when you choose to put others before yourself—when you put their needs before your own. You can allow someone to go before you in line. You can do work at home that others usually take care of. You can lay down your life simply by taking time out of your schedule for someone else.** Ask:

• **How can we put others before ourselves at school? at work? at home? at church?**

• **How will *you* follow Jesus' and Kolbe's examples this week?**

Service

Harriet Tubman (1820–1913)

Read the following true story aloud to your students, or ask a student to read it aloud.

When she was a young girl, Harriet Tubman was taken away from her mother because her master had decided to rent her out to another farm. Harriet sobbed as the wagon carried her away from her mother. "Be strong, child, and the good Lord will help you," her mother called.

When she came down with the measles, Harriet was returned to the farm where her mother lived. There she eventually began to work in the fields. One day, when she was working in the fields, Harriet saw a slave try to escape. A young man named Jim ran through the fields as his overseer pursued him. The overseer caught up to Jim as Harriet curiously followed.

"You, girl!" the overseer yelled to Harriet. "Hold that boy, and don't let him get away." The overseer took out his whip, but Harriet didn't move and Jim started to run again. The overseer was furious. He picked up a heavy lead weight and threw it at the runaway, but the weight missed Jim and hit Harriet in the head. Harriet eventually recovered from the wound. But the experience made her decide that she would one day escape to freedom.

Harriet's chance came one morning as she drove the mules and wagon to the woods. Harriet was met by a Quaker woman who had overheard that Harriet was going to be sold to the deep South. The Quaker woman was part of a system called the "underground railroad" that led slaves to freedom in the North. The woman gave Harriet directions to a house that served as a "station" on the underground railroad.

That night, Harriet ran away to the house. Once she reached it, "conductors" of the underground railroad helped guide Harriet on the treacherous journey to freedom. Exhausted and relieved, Harriet made it to Pennsylvania, where she found freedom. She knelt on the ground and with tears on her face prayed,

Sidelight

While Harriet Tubman worked on the underground railroad, slave owners posted a reward of forty thousand dollars for her capture. She was never caught.

"Thank you, Lord. You brought me safely here."

In spite of the tremendous danger she faced in the South as a runaway slave, Harriet Tubman decided to return to help others find the same freedom God had given her. She took nineteen trips back to the South and led more than three hundred slaves to freedom. She even returned twice to the very plantation she had escaped from. Along with many other slaves, Harriet led her own family to freedom. She became known as "Moses" to many slaves since she, like Moses, led her people out of captivity.

(Adapted from Go Free or Die: A Story About Harriet Tubman *by Jeri Ferris.)*

Discussion Starter

Read Ephesians 4:11-13 aloud. Say: **God gives us gifts so we can use them to help and serve others. God gave Harriet Tubman the gift of freedom. She used that gift to help others find the same freedom she had found. Harriet's example is so powerful because she risked the very gift God had given her to use it to help others.**

Ask:

- **What do you think of Harriet Tubman?**
- **What gifts has God given you?**
- **How can you use those gifts to serve others?**

Have students form trios. Say: **I'd like you to create your own personal service project. With your group, take turns explaining the gifts God has given you; then help each other think about how each person can use his or her gifts to serve others. Help each person come up with a personal service project, then end your group time by praying for each other regarding those service projects.**

Sidelight

During one of her trips back to the South, Harriet Tubman encountered John Stewart, her former master. Before she reached the plantation, Harriet bought two live chickens. As she saw John Stewart approaching her, she stooped over like an old woman, let the chickens go, and hobbled after them. Stewart laughed at the sight, not recognizing Harriet, and went on his way.

Simplicity

Charles H. Spurgeon (1834–1892)

Read the following true story aloud to your students, or ask a student to read it aloud.

Charles Spurgeon was raised as a Christian, but he had a difficult time overcoming his feelings of need for peace and freedom. These feelings began in his teenage years. He explained, "I was years and years upon the brink of hell—I mean in my own feeling. I was unhappy, I was desponding, I was despairing. My life was full of sorrow and wretchedness, believing that I was lost."

This feeling and attitude continued until Spurgeon was fifteen. He was on his way to his family church during a horrible snowstorm. The storm became so fierce that Spurgeon ducked into a different church for shelter. As he warmed himself in the back of the church, Spurgeon listened to a very inexperienced and untalented lay preacher at the pulpit. The man was teaching on Isaiah 45:22: "Turn to me and be saved, all you ends of the earth; for I am God, and there is no other."

Spurgeon explained the experience, "He had not much to say, thank God, for that compelled him to keep on repeating his text, and there was nothing needed—by me, at any rate—except his text. Then, stopping, he pointed to where I was sitting under the gallery, and he said, 'That young man there looks very miserable'...and he shouted..., 'Look! Look, young man! Look now!'...Then I had this vision—not a vision to my eyes, but to my heart. I saw what a Savior Christ was."

It was this simple and poorly prepared sermon that brought Spurgeon to Christ. Because of one man's willingness to simply and ineloquently give the message of salvation in Jesus, Charles Spurgeon became one of the most famous and effective preachers of all time.

(Adapted from Christian History magazine, Volume 10, Number 1.)

Discussion Starter

Say: **Charles Spurgeon told thousands of people about Jesus and encouraged countless Christians in their faith. He was one of the most witty and eloquent preachers of all time. But what would have happened if the inexperienced lay preacher had never mustered the courage to stand in front of the congregation and repeat the Scripture passage over and over? Maybe Charles Spurgeon never would have shared the message of Jesus with a single person. Maybe he never would have preached a single sermon.**

Have teenagers form a circle. Have each person share a time when a small event in his or her life made a big difference. Begin by sharing your own example.

After everyone has shared, read John 3:16 aloud. Say: **The message of the gospel is very simple, and so is your part in sharing the message. You may become the next Charles Spurgeon. But you're just as likely to share your faith with the next Charles Spurgeon or to encourage the next Charles Spurgeon when he or she feels like giving up. All you have to be is who God calls you to be—it's that simple.**

Strength

Brother Andrew (born 1928)

Read the following true story aloud to your students, or ask a student to read it aloud.

In 1957, Brother Andrew was preaching at a small church in Belgrade, Yugoslavia. The sermon seemed to be going well. So at the end of the sermon, Andrew asked the members of the congregation to raise their hands if they wanted to follow Jesus. All the people in the room raised their hands. Excited by the response, Andrew continued to challenge the congregation to pray and read their Bibles daily.

As he was preaching, Brother Andrew caught a concerned look from the church pastor. The Yugoslavian pastor whispered to Andrew, "Praying we can do. But reading the Bible? Andrew, these people don't have Bibles."

Shocked, Andrew asked the crowd if anyone had a Bible. Only seven people indicated they did. It was then that Andrew knew he must begin working to get God's Word into the hands of the people in communist countries. So Brother Andrew began smuggling Bibles behind the Iron Curtain.

Andrew explained the day-to-day work of smuggling Bibles: "From the outside, my work may have looked glamorous, but inside, it was a daily struggle. I was in a new mission field, so there was no one to ask for advice, no one to keep me from making mistakes...I had a serious problem with a slipped disc and was always tired, sick, and in pain. I was lonely and very poor."

Sidelight

Brother Andrew and his workers smuggled one million Bibles into China in a single night!

But Andrew kept smuggling Bibles—even in the midst of overwhelming fear. Andrew told about a few of his experiences with fear: "I've driven toward the Iron Curtain with my carload of Scripture, arrived at the border, seen the controls, and gotten so scared I've turned around and driven back to a hotel in the nearest village where I could pray and fast. I'd stay there until I had faith that with God I was a majority."

Brother Andrew's strength and persistence led to Bible-smuggling throughout the world, including China, Africa, Central America, and the Middle East. Through his efforts, millions of Bibles have reached people who otherwise would have had no access to the Word of God.

(Adapted from More Than Conquerors: Portraits of Believers From All Walks of Life, *edited by John Woodbridge.)*

Discussion Starter

Have teenagers form four groups. Explain that you're going to have each group do a different test of strength. Some of the students may be able to complete some of the tests of strength. But many students will not. Ask the first group:

• **Do you think you can touch the floor while keeping your bottom and your heels against the wall?**

Have all the members of the first group put their backs against the wall and attempt to touch the floor while keeping their bottoms and their heels against the wall. Then ask the second group:

• **Do you think you can fold a sheet of paper in half nine times?**

Give each member of the second group a sheet of paper, and have the group members attempt to fold the sheets in half nine times. Then ask the third group:

• **Do you think you can eat a piece of bread in a minute or less?**

Give each member of the third group a piece of dry bread. Don't let the teenagers drink anything. Let them know when a minute is up. Then ask the fourth group:

• **Do you think you can crush a raw egg in the palm of your hand?**

Give each member of the fourth group a raw egg, and have teenagers try to crush the eggs in one hand over a trash can. Tell the students they must completely cover the eggs in their palms and they must try to squeeze the eggs rather than putting pressure on the eggs with their fingertips.

Ask:

• **What about the tests of strength surprised you?**
• **Do you consider yourself to be a strong person?**
• **Are you as strong as Brother Andrew? Explain.**

Read 2 Corinthians 12:9-10. Say: **You may or may not be able to crush an egg or fold a piece of paper. But without God, none of us have the strength to do anything that's truly worthwhile. Brother Andrew knew that God was his source of strength. When he was afraid, he prayed and fasted. God is our strength, and with him everything and anything is possible.**

Trust

Hudson Taylor (1832–1905)

Read the following true story aloud to your students, or ask a student to read it aloud.

At seventeen, Hudson Taylor knew he was called to go to China. He trained himself by studying medicine under his uncle, who was a doctor. To prepare himself, Taylor purposely lived in poverty. Taylor once even gave his last coin to a starving woman, not knowing how he would pay for the meals of the next day. Soon afterward, he received an anonymous gift of more money than he had given away!

At the age of twenty-one, Taylor left for China, where he worked as a missionary for six years. Just as Taylor began reaching deeper and deeper parts of China, he became ill and had to take his family back to London. But Taylor couldn't find peace while he was in London. He couldn't bear the thought of "a million a month dying in the land without God."

Taylor tried to get missionary societies to support his efforts, but none of them would. He knew that if he were going back to China, he would have to start his own mission. But the thought of bringing other people into the dangers of China overwhelmed him. He could trust God for himself, but trusting God for others was another matter.

Taylor's unfulfilled dream brought him close to a nervous breakdown. Then one morning as he walked on the beach, he looked at the sea and the sky and noticed God's glory, beauty, and splendor. He thought, "If God gives us a band of men for Inland China, and they go, and all die of starvation even, they will only be taken straight to heaven. And if one...soul is saved would it not be worthwhile? Why, if we are obeying the Lord, the responsibility rests with him, not with us." Taylor prayed for twenty-four people to go with him to China.

Sidelight

Even though his father, mother, and sister were strong Christians, Hudson Taylor rejected the faith of his upbringing until he was seventeen. Taylor became a Christian after reading a tract about a man who believed his sins stopped him from reaching Christ.

Eleven months later, Taylor, his wife, and seventeen others sailed for China. The other missionaries of his group had gone before or were soon to follow. The group started the China Inland Mission, which later became the largest single Protestant body in China.

(Adapted from More Than Conquerors: Portraits of Believers From All Walks of Life, *edited by John Woodbridge.)*

Discussion Starter

Ask:

• **Why do you think Hudson Taylor had such a difficult time trusting that God would take care of the people he wanted to bring to China with him?**

• **Do you agree with the reasons Taylor came up with for trusting God? Explain.**

• **What is significant about the time Taylor gave the coin to the poor woman?**

• **Do you trust God?**

• **How do you know you can trust God?**

Ask teenagers to hold their breath. While teenagers are holding their breath, ask:

• **How many of you trust that there will be air to breathe once you stop holding your breath?**

Tell students to resume breathing, and ask teenagers to close their eyes. While everyone's eyes are closed, ask:

• **How many of you trust that you'll see the sun tomorrow?**

• **How many of you trust that when you go through a green light, the cars coming the other way will stop at the red light?**

• **How many of you trust that your friends will still be your friends tomorrow?**

Tell students to open their eyes, and then read Proverbs 3:5-6 aloud. Say: **I'm more convinced that God will always be there for you and that you can trust God than I'm certain that the sun will come up tomorrow. I have greater trust that God will provide for my needs than I do that air will be available for my next breath. God has an eternal track record. God has always been trustworthy and has always kept his Word. Since Creation, God has faithfully watched over**

Sidelight

At the time of Hudson Taylor's death in 1905, the China Inland Mission had 205 stations with 849 missionaries, and 125,000 Chinese Christians were in the China Inland Mission.

his children. Understand that God may not do things the way you expect, but God will always be with you and you can always trust in God—more than you can trust anything or anyone else.

Truth

C.S. Lewis (1898–1963)

Read the following true story aloud to your students, or ask a student to read it aloud.

The story of how C.S. Lewis became a Christian is especially noteworthy because he spent much of his young adulthood as an atheist. As a young child, C.S. Lewis had lived in a warm and happy home. His entire family devoured books, and they were all members of the Church of Ireland. Lewis had a very special relationship with his mother. But when Lewis was only nine years old, tragedy struck his family—his mother died of cancer. The event changed Lewis' view of God. He figured God either was cruel or didn't exist. The disillusion eventually turned into atheism.

Lewis' return to Christianity didn't happen with a flood of emotion, a dramatic prayer, or a penetrating sermon. His first step toward Christianity came from a simple conversation with a philosophy teacher at Magdalen College. Lewis respected the opinion of the teacher very much. Both men were very interested in folklore and magic and talked about the subjects for some time. Lewis argued that people turned to religion after they found that magic and folklore failed. The teacher basically argued that Christianity was true. Lewis was surprised to find that the man was a Christian, and the conversation unbolted the door to his heart.

The next step occurred when Lewis was riding on a bus. He had been reading great Christian authors such as Edmund Spenser and John Milton and books of philosophy such as *Space, Time, and Deity.* As he was riding on the bus, he thought about all he had read. He didn't believe in God when he got on the bus—by the time the bus reached Lewis' stop, he believed some sort of absolute being probably did exist.

Sidelight

C.S. Lewis died November 22, 1963—the same day as John F. Kennedy and Aldous Huxley, author of *Brave New World.*

Shortly after the bus trip, Lewis was brought closer to the truth of Christianity when he examined his own heart. An honest look at himself revealed that he had hate, lust, and fear hidden within. He was confronted with the truth of who he was, and rather than explaining it away or justifying himself, Lewis accepted the truth and let it sink into his heart. The experience frightened and changed him. He explained, "I gave in, and admitted that God was God, and knelt and prayed: perhaps, that night, the most dejected and reluctant convert in all England."

Lewis began to ask questions about God and Christianity. Fortunately, J.R.R. Tolkien and H.V. Dyson were there to provide answers. Lewis spent many long walks asking the men about truth and Christian doctrine and beliefs. Lewis finally fully accepted Christianity on a motorcycle ride to the zoo. His talks with Tolkien and Dyson were swirling in his head. When he arrived at the zoo, he believed that Jesus was the Son of God. It was an amazing revelation for a man who once had been an ardent atheist.

(Adapted from More Than Conquerors: Portraits of Believers From All Walks of Life, *edited by John Woodbridge, and Christian History magazine, Volume 4, Number 3.)*

Discussion Starter

Before this devotion, meet with three teenagers from your group. Appoint one person to prepare to tell a true story that happened in his or her life. Have each of the other two teenagers prepare to tell stories that sound believable but didn't really happen.

Have the three teenagers sit at the front of the room. Have the remaining students form two or three groups. Say: **Each of these three people is going to tell you a story. One of the stories will be true. The other two will be made up. After the stories, each group can ask one question of each person to gather more information. Then you'll guess which person you think is telling the truth. The only question you can't ask is "Is your story true?"**

Sidelight

An animated version of *The Lion, the Witch & the Wardrobe,* written by C.S. Lewis, has been viewed by more than 35 million people.

Have the three teenagers tell their stories. Then allow each group to ask one question of each storyteller.

Ask groups to guess which person is telling the truth; then have the storytellers reveal which story is real.

Ask:

• **How can you tell when something is true?**
• **How did C.S. Lewis find the truth?**

Give volunteers an opportunity to share their own stories about how they became Christians or how they discovered one of God's truths. After teenagers have had a chance to share, read Matthew 7:7-8 aloud. Say: **Sometimes understanding truth is quick and apparent—God just makes it plain. Sometimes we have to seek and struggle just as C.S. Lewis did. It's OK to struggle with some of the things you hear about God and the world. But it's essential that you look for the truth in those situations. Check the Bible, talk with mature Christians, and pray for God's wisdom. According to God's timing, God will show you the truth.**

Sidelight

J.R.R. Tolkien criticized C.S. Lewis' *Chronicles of Narnia.* He thought the books were too unrealistic and hastily written.

Understanding
Francis of Assisi (1181–1226)

Read the following true story aloud to your students, or ask a student to read it aloud.

Francis of Assisi was born to a wealthy textile merchant in 1181. Francis was given all the comforts, privileges, and schooling that a wealthy merchant's son could expect. But after fighting in a war against Perugia, Francis began to question his wealth and the meaning of his own existence.

So Francis went on a pilgrimage to Rome to find himself. He knew what it meant to be rich and self-centered, so he decided to find out what it meant to be poor and dedicated to God. So while Francis was in Rome, he exchanged his merchant clothes for the clothes of a beggar.

The experience changed the way Francis looked at poverty and suffering. Living like a beggar gave him compassion and understanding for the poor. Rather than looking at the poor as lesser people, Francis understood that they were human and in need of help.

So Francis reconstructed one of the city's churches and began ministering to the outcasts of society. He sold his horse and some of his father's merchandise to raise the necessary support.

Sidelight

In his desire to become closer to Christ, Francis of Assisi left the order he had started and went to a hermitage (or a monastery) for solitude and prayer.

Francis' father was outraged at his son's seemingly wasteful actions. Francis' father didn't understand his son's desire to help the poor and saw Francis' actions as wasteful. So he had Francis brought before the bishop, where Francis was ordered to return all he had taken from his father. Francis responded by stripping himself naked and returning the property and clothing to his father. Then Francis denied his father, exclaiming that God alone was his father.

Francis immediately went to work (after clothing himself) caring for victims of leprosy. He gained a small following that concentrated on understanding and helping the poor and oppressed. The group was recognized by the pope and became an official Catholic order. The men of the order had no possessions and spent their days "announcing the kingdom of God," praying, helping others, and living in poverty.

(Adapted from Great Leaders of the Christian Church, *edited by John D. Woodbridge.)*

Discussion Starter

Ask:

• **Why do you think Francis' dad had such little understanding of Francis' choices?**

• **When have you ever felt misunderstood? Explain.**

• **Why do you think Francis had so much understanding and compassion for the poor and suffering?**

• **Do you have the same understanding and compassion? Why or why not?**

Give each student a sheet of paper and a pen or pencil. Say: **Create a person who is exactly unlike you. On the top of your paper write his or her name. Then list all the things that make him or her different from you. For example, the person should have a different race and gender and different interests. When you're finished, find a partner and tell your partner what you think it would be like to be your fictional character.**

As partners begin talking, ask them to discuss these questions:

• **What struggles would your fictional characters have? what concerns?**

• **What things would interest your fictional characters?**

• **What motivates your characters?**

• **If your fictional character wasn't a Christian, how would you go about telling him or her about Jesus?**

Have pairs read 1 Corinthians 9:19-23. Say: **It's natural to want to be around people who are similar to you. But God wants us to reach out to everyone—including those who are very different from us. It's easy to judge or exclude people who are different. But when we spend**

Sidelight

The men who joined the order established by Francis of Assisi were required to "live in obedience, in chastity and without property, following the teaching and footsteps of our Lord Jesus Christ."

time with those people, we find that they have value and that they're important to God. We need to make an effort to understand and reach out to people who are different—just as Francis of Assisi did.

Wisdom

Tom Maharias (born 1949)

Read the following true story aloud to your students, or ask a student to read it aloud.

When he was eight years old, Tom Maharias and his family emigrated from Greece to New York. In New York, Tom wasn't well-accepted by the kids in his neighborhood—they flattened his bike tires, threatened him, and taunted him. In his New York neighborhood, Tom learned not to trust others, and he learned to be tough.

As Tom grew into adulthood, he became heavily involved in the hippie lifestyle. He and his girlfriend, Vicky, moved into their friends' apartment in Greenwich Village. They explored various religions and got heavily involved in the drug scene. Once, while tripping on LSD, they ran through Central Park, asking people, "Who are we? Where did we come from? Why are we here? Where are we going?"

Tom ended up in a psychiatric hospital, where he was diagnosed as schizophrenic. After his release, Tom was surprised when a young man walked up to him and asked if he could talk to him about God and spirituality. Suspicious and overwhelmed, Tom accused the man of being Satan. The young man calmly responded to Tom's accusation by saying, "No, I'm Bruce."

Most people would have responded to Tom's paranoid attitude and remarks by ending the conversation and getting away. Instead, this particular man reacted with amazing wisdom and serenity. Bruce's calm and wise response took Tom off guard and gave Bruce an opportunity to speak into his life. Bruce spent the next two hours answering Tom's questions by pointing him to various Scripture passages.

Bruce then invited Tom to a Christian retreat center, where Tom asked God for forgiveness and committed his life to Jesus. Tom's life changed from that point on. He became a pastor of Manhattan

Sidelight

In high school, Tom Maharias was rebellious and heavily involved in drugs. Two months before graduating from George Washington High School, he was expelled for getting into a fistfight with the principal.

Bible Church. Through the church, Tom has developed a number of programs to help the people of New York and to train people to share the gospel around the world. The wisdom of an obscure man named Bruce truly turned Tom's life around.

(Adapted from Ambassadors for Christ: Distinguished Representatives of the Message Throughout the World, *edited by John D. Woodbridge.)*

Discussion Starter

Say: **Bruce responded to Tom Maharias in a way that was much different than most people would have. Most people would have wanted to get as far away as possible from an apparently crazy man who called them Satan. But Bruce had the wisdom to calmly get through Tom's defenses. Because of Bruce's reaction, he had the opportunity to tell Tom about Jesus.**

Read 1 Corinthians 3:18-20 aloud.

Have teenagers form trios. Say: **God's wisdom is very different from what the world thinks is wise or important. True wisdom is found in Scripture and in understanding what God wants us to do. I'm going to list a few areas of life. For each area of life, work with your group to decide what the world or society thinks about it and what God thinks about it.** Give groups time to talk about each of the following areas:

Sidelight

Tom Maharias shared his faith with his girlfriend, Vicky. She became a Christian, and the two were later married.

- money
- relationships
- spirituality
- happiness

Have groups share what they discussed regarding each area. Then ask:

- **What's the difference between God's wisdom and the wisdom of this world?**
- **How do we gain wisdom?**

Close the devotion in prayer, asking God to bless each teenager with the wisdom of God.

Scripture Index

General Index

Group Publishing, Inc.
Attention: Product Development
P.O. Box 481
Loveland, CO 80539
Fax: (970) 679-4370

Evaluation for *CHARACTER COUNTS!*

Please help Group Publishing, Inc., continue to provide innovative and useful resources for ministry. Please take a moment to fill out this evaluation and mail or fax it to us. Thanks!

● ● ●

1. As a whole, this book has been (circle one)

not very helpful   very helpful

1   2   3   4   5   6   7   8   9   10

2. The best things about this book:

3. Ways this book could be improved:

4. Things I will change because of this book:

5. Other books I'd like to see Group publish in the future:

6. Would you be interested in field-testing future Group products and giving us your feedback? If so, please fill in the information below:

Name _____

Street Address _____

City _____ State _____ ZIP _____

Phone Number _____ Date _____

Bible Study Series

Give Your Teenagers a Solid Faith Foundation That Lasts a Lifetime!

Here are the *essentials* of the Christian life—core values teenagers *must* believe to make good decisions now...and build an *unshakable* lifelong faith. Developed by youth workers like you...field-tested with *real* youth groups in *real* churches...here's the meat your kids *must* have to grow spiritually—presented in a fun, involving way!

Each 4-session **Core Belief Bible Study Series** book lets you easily...

● Lead deep, compelling, *relevant* discussions your kids won't want to miss...
● Involve teenagers in exploring life-changing truths...
● Help kids create healthy relationships with each other—and you!

Plus you'll make an *eternal difference* in the lives of your kids as you give them a solid faith foundation that stands firm on God's Word.

Here are the Core Belief Bible Study Series titles already available...

Senior High Studies

Why **Authority** Matters	0-7644-0892-5
Why **Being a Christian** Matters	0-7644-0883-6
Why **Creation** Matters	0-7644-0880-1
Why **Forgiveness** Matters	0-7644-0887-9
Why **God** Matters	0-7644-0874-7
Why **God's Justice** Matters	0-7644-0886-0
Why **Jesus Christ** Matters	0-7644-0875-5
Why **Love** Matters	0-7644-0889-5
Why **Our Families** Matter	0-7644-0894-1
Why **Personal Character** Matters	0-7644-0885-2
Why **Prayer** Matters	0-7644-0893-3
Why **Relationships** Matter	0-7644-0896-8
Why **Serving Others** Matters	0-7644-0895-X
Why **Spiritual Growth** Matters	0-7644-0884-4
Why **Suffering** Matters	0-7644-0879-8
Why **the Bible** Matters	0-7644-0882-8
Why **the Church** Matters	0-7644-0890-9
Why **the Holy Spirit** Matters	0-7644-0876-3
Why **the Last Days** Matter	0-7644-0888-7
Why **the Spiritual Realm** Matters	0-7644-0881-X
Why **Worship** Matters	0-7644-0891-7

Junior High/Middle School Studies

The Truth About **Authority**	0-7644-0868-2
The Truth About **Being a Christian**	0-7644-0859-3
The Truth About **Creation**	0-7644-0856-9
The Truth About **Developing Character**	0-7644-0861-5
The Truth About **God**	0-7644-0850-X
The Truth About **God's Justice**	0-7644-0862-3
The Truth About **Jesus Christ**	0-7644-0851-8
The Truth About **Love**	0-7644-0865-8
The Truth About **Our Families**	0-7644-0870-4
The Truth About **Prayer**	0-7644-0869-0
The Truth About **Relationships**	0-7644-0872-0
The Truth About **Serving Others**	0-7644-0871-2
The Truth About **Sin and Forgiveness**	0-7644-0863-1
The Truth About **Spiritual Growth**	0-7644-0860-7
The Truth About **Suffering**	0-7644-0855-0
The Truth About **the Bible**	0-7644-0858-5
The Truth About **the Church**	0-7644-0899-2
The Truth About **the Holy Spirit**	0-7644-0852-6
The Truth About **the Last Days**	0-7644-0864-X
The Truth About **the Spiritual Realm**	0-7644-0857-7
The Truth About **Worship**	0-7644-0867-4

Exciting Resources for Your Youth Ministry

All-Star Games From All-Star Youth Leaders

The ultimate game book—from the biggest names in youth ministry! All-time no-fail favorites from Wayne Rice, Les Christie, Rich Mullins, Tiger McLuen, Darrell Pearson, Dave Stone, Bart Campolo, Steve Fitzhugh, and 21 others! You get all the games you'll need for any situation. Plus, you get practical advice about how to design your own games and tricks for turning a *good* game into a *great* game!

ISBN 0-7644-2020-8

Last Impressions: Unforgettable Closings for Youth Meetings

Make the closing moments of your youth programs powerful and memorable with this collection of Group's best-ever low-prep (or no-prep!) youth meeting closings. You get over 170 favorite closings, each tied to a thought-provoking Bible passage. Great for anyone who works with teenagers!

ISBN 1-55945-629-9

The Youth Worker's Encyclopedia of Bible-Teaching Ideas

Here are the most comprehensive idea-books available for youth workers. With more than 365 creative ideas in each of these 400-page encyclopedias, there's at least one idea for every book of the Bible. You'll find ideas for retreats and overnighters...learning games... adventures...special projects...affirmations...parties...prayers...music... devotions...skits...and more!

Old Testament   ISBN 1-55945-184-X
New Testament   ISBN 1-55945-183-1

PointMaker™ Devotions for Youth Ministry

These 45 PointMakers™ help your teenagers discover, understand, and apply biblical principles. Use PointMakers as brief meetings on specific topics or slide them into any youth curriculum to make a lasting impression. Includes handy Scripture and topical indexes that make it quick and easy to select the perfect PointMaker for any lesson you want to teach!

ISBN 0-7644-2003-8

More Resources for Your Youth Ministry

Group's Best Discussion Launchers for Youth Ministry

Here's the definitive collection of Group's best-ever discussion launchers! You'll get hundreds of thought-provoking questions kids can't resist discussing...compelling quotes that demand a response...and quick activities that pull kids into an experience they can't wait to talk about. Add zing to your youth meetings...revive meetings that are drifting off-track...and comfortably approach sensitive topics like AIDS, war, cults, gangs, suicide, dating, parents, self-image, and more!

ISBN 0-7644-2023-2

You-Choose-the-Ending Skits for Youth Ministry

Stephen Parolini

Try these 19 hot-topic skits guaranteed to keep your kids on the edge of their seats—because each skit has 3 possible endings! You can choose the ending...flip a coin...or let your teenagers vote. No matter which ending you pick, you'll get a great discussion going about a topic kids care about! Included: no-fail discussion questions!

ISBN 1-55945-627-2

No Supplies Required Crowdbreakers & Games

Dan McGill

This is the perfect book for youth workers on a tight budget. The only supplies you'll need for these quick activities are kids! All 95 ideas are fun, easy-to-do, creative, and tested for guaranteed success!

ISBN 1-55945-700-7

Youth Worker's Idea Depot™

Practical, proven ideas gathered from front-line professionals make this CD-ROM a gold mine of ministry solutions! You can search these ideas instantly—by Scripture...topic...key words...or by personal notes you've entered into your database. You'll get a complete library of ideas—plus a trial subscription to Group Magazine, where you'll discover dozens of new ideas in every issue! For Windows 3.1 or Windows 95.

ISBN 0-7644-2034-8